Pastor Clint is concerned about feeding people. Not feeding us bullshit. And that's pretty awesome. Read this book. It's really [fucking] good.

—Tom Gaulke, author of *Everyday Armageddons* (Pickwick, 2023)

Through theory and experiences, and in the context the challenging context of a reactionary southern culture I know well, Schnekloth gives a glimpse of something redeeming. His deep care for the vulnerable is evident on every page.

—Tad DeLay, author of *Future of Denial: The Ideologies of Climate Change* (Verson, 2024)

Drawing from the experiences of a radically left Lutheran church in the American South, Schnekloth shares thought- and action-provoking stories for those who care deeply about their communities and who are seeking meaningful ways to integrate their faith and make a difference in ways beyond the obvious.

—Victoria Goddard, author of *The Hands of the Emperor* and other fantasy novels

Schnekloth's guidebook is an invitation into a Christian tradition that is both unflinchingly ever-evolving (as the specifics of what it looks like to be Christ in the world changes) and unashamedly adherent to the best parts of tradition and orthodoxy. For those coming from mainstream conservative evangelical traditions or simply seeking a primer on what it looks like to be both leftist and Christian, this guidebook provides a window into progressive Christian belief and community through the fun and inspiring stories of a congregation blazing a trail in the US south.

—Trinity McMahan, member of Good Shepherd Lutheran Church, Arkansas

A GUIDEBOOK TO
PROGRESSIVE CHURCH

A GUIDEBOOK TO
PROGRESSIVE CHURCH

CLINT SCHNEKLOTH

CONTENTS

To the people of Good Shepherd Lutheran Church, Fayetteville, Arkansas

FOREWORD

If you had asked me in the early 1990's at Luther College to look around at my fellow English majors and campus ministry colleagues and predict which one would write a book on progressive Christianity, I would not have answered, "Clint Schnekloth."

I can't point to a specific incident, but rather just a general frustration with Clint, both in classes and around campus ministry. In classes, he seemed like he'd rather be in conversation with the professor than bother with the rest of us undergrads. In campus ministry, he was too traditional, too judgmental. I thought of Clint as one of those people who seemed to know everything, yet nothing at all.

But something started to change for Clint (and others) during our time at Luther. In the Spring of 1993, a busload of 40 people from our college headed to the March on Washington for Lesbian, Gay, and Bi Equal Rights and Liberation. Inspired by the experience, a few folks in campus ministry started to discuss becoming a community that affirmed LGBTQ people. Clint listened to the conversations and leaned into his friendships with LGBTQ people. The next year, Clint led the process to become Reconciling in Christ, the official designation in our Lutheran denomination for LGBTQ affirming congregations. Around that same time, I started drifting from the church, frustrated by the continued patriarchal and institutional church. We graduated and went our separate ways.

Clint went into specialized and then parish ministry. A couple years into his third call, Clint's congregation faced a deep divide over same-sex marriage. Clint stuck with the gays. Half of his congregation left to form a new community. Clint's congregation started to rebuild. Around that time, Clint and I reconnected via the internet and ministry. I was working with an organization that supported publicly identifying LGBTQ+ people called to ministry in the Lutheran church. Soon, I was reading about all kinds of work that Clint was leading. His congregation created and launched Queer Camp, a summer camp for LGBTQ+ youth. In Arkansas. Next, Clint's congregation had started opening their doors to refugees, eventually creating a new organization, Canopy Northwest Arkansas, that has served over 700 individuals who have settled in Northwest Arkansas.

As my path has led me back into the heart of organized Lutheranism (seminary, call process, serving as a pastor), Clint's path has been leading him to the edges of Christianity. It's like we handed off batons at some point. This past spring I was co-chairing a bishop election committee while Clint was writing blog posts questioning the purpose of bishops. All the while, we have stayed in regular communication, sometimes publicly disagreeing on Facebook, sometimes privately debating over text messages or a phone call, but always staying in conversation. I have always been amazed by how prolific Clint is. Every so often, Clint texts me with a question or thought. Two hours later, I'm still pondering the question, and Clint has published a 500-word essay on the topic. It probably took me longer to write this foreword than it took him to write the book.

All of this leads me to Clint's book, *A Guidebook to Progressive Church,* which captures his expansive, active, and just ahead of the moment mind. I imagine Clint up late at night or early in the morning, pondering how to faithfully lead his community forward. And as I've read his blogs and Facebook posts, and traded text messages, and then read this book, I realized that I felt true and deep affection for Clint. Not a well-we've-known-each-other-forever palship. Affection. Kinship. The kind of relationship he is always seeking to create is the kind of ministry he describes in *A Guidebook.*

In the first section, *Invitation,* Clint addresses questions about the descriptor "progressive," provides instruction for wandering would-be progressive Christians, takes a detailed dive into a particularly progressive Christian experience (spoiler: it is queer-friendly and there are tarot cards).

Keywords. Clint digs more deeply into some specific areas in the second section. I resonated deeply with the chapter on discipleship. Clint asks if it is "cringy," and I was hoping his conclusion was not because we just added a pastoral role for discipleship in my current context (he offers a non-cringy approach to discipleship). His geeky exploration of *Freidigkeit* (brazen freedom) is what many of us need right now—to get past getting along to get along and instead to move "into bold forms of truth, in action and speech" (p. 55). Clint's words on taking risks are convicting and energizing.

Next, Clint explores *Intersections*. Delving into the topics of feminism, neurodivergence, queer virtue, and respectability culture, he opens the conversation even further—into places that many "all are welcome" congregations fear to tread. In his chapter on "Women's Work," I would add this to his list of the church tasks dominated by women: assisting ministers, communion servers, ushers, visiting ministers, council, and committee chairs.

The fourth section, *Belief*, will provide excellent conversation material for anyone who wants to argue that progressive Christianity is a theologically vacuous do-gooder club. Clint gets into atheism, the Nicene Creed, Biblical interpretation, and then some. For those wanting a deeper exploration, he shares resources to do so. For those who need language to claim how central faith and God's word are to the progressive Christian, Clint offers words like this: "We hold the Scriptures lightly for the same reason we hold the hands of our family members lightly. Because we love them" (p.111).

Finally, *Praxis* and *Polis*. How does this all work? And to what end? In these final sections, Clint explores a range of ways progressive Christians can engage others and the world. He issues the warning that "one of the greatest dangers of progressive Christianity, is a tendency toward performative gestures at justice rather than sacrificial commitment to justice itself" (140). He is honest about what the path forward, what it might look like, how to take steps in the direction of justice, and the importance of confession, forgiveness, courage and Christ in the process.

What I find most valuable in this book is what I've found to be true about Clint over the 30+ years that we've known each other—he values and grounds his work in relationship, is open to change, stays in the conversation. Whether you are convinced by or curious about progressive church, I commend this book to you.

Amalia Vagts

ACKNOWLEDGMENTS

The communities who formed me inspired this book, including congregations in such far-flung locales as Davenport, Iowa, Washington D.C., Twin Cities, Minnesota, rural Wisconsin, Košice, Slovakia, and Northwest Arkansas.

Campus and camp ministries were also influential, especially time at Luther College in Decorah, Iowa and Luther Seminary in St. Paul, Minnesota.

My intellectual debts are to a wide array of authors, reflected in the further reading notes.

This book would not exist without the passionate support of a few people. When I was paused at the publishing stage and wondering whether I wanted to move forward, Victoria Goddard stepped up offering tremendous editing and formatting support.

When I sent an early draft out to readers, Lisa Hinrichson dropped everything and read the book in two days, taking copious notes, and the final order of chapters (and a few new chapters) are thanks to her energy.

For a Kickstarter, you need a cover, and I love the work of Alysa May. The signs outside our church, including the fantastic Here Be Dragons sign (which is now also a Pokestop) are her design, and I knew I wanted her to create this cover.

Trinity McMahan, Tom Gaulke, Tad DeLay, and an array of friends offered comment on individual chapters and blurbs for the book. Thank you!

Amalia Vagts has been a close confidante and friend through the making of this book, and in so many other ways, and I love her personable foreword.

My family has mostly grown used to the pauses that happen when, after a jog or early morning inspiration, I have to sit down and write out thoughts that had been coalescing, and I thank them for their patience and love.

Finally, I'd like to acknowledge all those at the front lines practicing progressive church, including my own congregation here in Fayetteville who has been on this progressive adventure with me for over fourteen years. To the many friends and co-conspirators, you know who you are. Thanks especially to our church staff, who I've frequently bounced ideas off of.

Progressive church is a movement, and movements are about relationships and growing together. Thank you to all those who are in this work.

INTRODUCTION

A few years ago, I was driving down to Little Rock to participate in the Poor Peoples' Campaign at a rally at the capitol. Midway we stopped at a McDonalds. I was wearing a rainbow clerical collar handmade by some members of the church. A woman from a small coffee group approached and asked, "What does your collar mean?"

Me, internally: "Uh oh."

Me, externally: "Well, my people made it for me because we love queer people so much and want to show it."

Her: "Oh my."

Then a quick turn on her heels and exit in a huff.

These days, if I can get away with it, I prefer to just show up at protests without the clerical shirt. I've become a kind of Quaker Lutheran, less interested in claiming or exhibiting a distinction between clergy and laity. I guess it helps that a lot of people know me. I moved to Arkansas over a dozen years ago from the Midwest and have stuck around. But at the most recent protest (in defense of reproductive rights), I showed up not with a collar but bottles of water and a big jug of sweet tea and cups. After all the gospel of Matthew emphasizes Christians are to offer a cup of water to their neighbor and doesn't say anything at all about special shirts for the priests.

I've become ambivalent about the clerics, but I do believe in showing up, and sometimes doing so with visibility. For many people today there is rather limited exposure to the presence of Christian progressive pastors. Numerically, at least here in Arkansas, we're a very distinct minority. But we're here, and because we see our calling as progressive Christians as connected to social justice and even political issues in God's world, you come across us especially advocating and acting at justice intersections, and then you have to attempt to reconcile our Christianity with, well, the rest of Christianity more frequently seen on the news. Those on the left may be much less likely to cross the threshold of our churches on a Sunday morning, but they have come to anticipate that we serve (a little like a beautiful unicorn appearing in the woods on a moonlit evening) as quasi-chaplains in progressive spaces.

Speaking of shirts, however, my friend and colleague handmakes Marshallese shirts I like to wear. They aren't clerics, they're Marshallese. The style among Marshallese is to design a large batch of matching dresses and shirts for special occasions, like first birthdays or weddings. My favorite is one he made for me at the launch of Ozark Atolls, our ministry accompanying the Marshallese community in Northwest Arkansas. It's light-blue bespoke with a stretch of rainbow across the upper right shoulder. I love wearing it first of all because I look really good in it, and I get a lot of compliments. But I also love wearing it because it reminds me of how awkward the whole cross-cultural ministry gig can get.

A white male pastor wearing a Marshallese shirt could be (and on some levels inevitably is) engaging in cultural appropriation. I'm continually frustrated that one of the early organizing rules our Marshallese community director Albious learned from his dad was, "If you want to get something done, get a white person to speak up for you about it." I don't know if I'm most frustrated that his dad was and remains right, or that I'm complicit in it because sometimes for lack of a better solution we still repeat that pattern. But I wear the shirt first of all because it was made for me by my friend, and he wants me to wear it, and then also because in wearing it, I'm reminded of how much anti-racism work I still have to do, together with my community, to truly deserve wearing the shirt, if "deserve" is even the right term here. So far the best thing we've done as a church in recent years is open our space to the Marshallese community—many days it seems like we are as much a Marshallese community center as a Lutheran church. I'm cool with that, because it's mutual.

I love progressive pastoring at least in part because it's inevitably situated in the bustle of complexities like these. There's a constant joke among clergy, "They didn't teach us that in seminary." It's a moderately funny joke that is probably unfair to what any graduate program can do to prepare someone for the life of Christian discipleship.

How could any seminary program designed in the 20th century have prepared a pastor to serve in a congregation in Arkansas that weekly partners with the largest Marshallese community outside the Marshall Islands itself, while simultaneously hosting a summer Queer Camp for LGBTQIA+ youth, and a Rainbow Closet that provides gender-affirming apparel for those in transition? I mean, not too long ago I had a very open conversation right away on a Monday morning about gender-affirming tucking undergarments before heading off to take communion to a centenarian in an assisted-living facility. By any measure, that's quite a range.

I mention all of this simply to whet your appetite for what I hope to do in this guidebook. I want to invite anyone who reads this book to imagine the journey that might take them from where they are currently (disenfranchised, belief-fluid, profoundly skeptical, traumatized but seeking, just plain curious, angry and disappointed) in and through the life of a local progressive Christian congregation (which I imagine might actually have parallels in the journey of connection to progressive synagogues, mosques, temples, etc.). Ultimately, I am offering an invitation to community, and will be doing so unapologetically (okay, actually quite apologetically because many apologies are needed to those who have been traumatized by religious community) because I truly believe it is the organizing power of local progressive communities of faith, warts and all, that stands the best chance of offering a coherent and life-giving alternative to those things that trouble us—things like neoliberalism, Christofascism, and climate change. Lots of books have been written on them all, and you can find references to some of them in the "For Further Reading" that concludes each chapter. My goal in this book will be to simply provide a lens from one perspective to life in my church, a progressive Christian church in the South, all in the hopes that such a guidebook will help you, your local DSA chapter, or your religious trauma support group consider communities of faith as, well, yours.

—

The book you hold in your hands is gathered from occasional writings. This fact accounts for a bit of messiness regarding tone and voice. As I have been at work on this guidebook, the inherent tension between literary coherence and practical application has been top of mind. As a pastor I write a lot, but almost everything I write is occasional and for specific contexts. Rarely if ever do I get far enough away from the nitty gritty of parish and community life to gain a bird's eye view.

There's a gambit here. I'm offering you, the reader, a glimpse directly into the mess, what is said and thought and tried in the weeks and months and years of practicing progressive church. What is gathered here is neither academically refined like a dissertation nor constructed in a coherent narrative like a memoir. Instead, this book finds its home more in the space of blogs and social media posts and sermons. Each chapter is a sort of intervention.

A comparison to collections of letters may be in order. I've always loved reading "Letters" because they provide such direct access to the authors. Unlike the polished prose of published works, letters tend to give us a glimpse into the room where the letters were written, right down to the wear and tear on the desk where they were written and the inner insecurities (and sometimes tears) of the author. But the strength of collected letters is also related to a simple editorial fact: the author did not write them for a book, they wrote them to a friend, a colleague, a lover. Gathered into a collection of letters, they retain their shape even while shaped into a more literary document.

So I have asked myself to what degree the chapters in this book should also retain their shape as occasional pieces, and I think you'll find they do. I've attempted to make them somewhat less confessional, more addressed *to* you than *by* me, and gathered up into topical sections. It is a guidebook, after all. But here again I think readers of a guidebook, though looking for actual insight into how to practice progressive church (or find their way to it), are also seeking models of how it's been tried. Emphasis on tried, because one of the admissions I make in the book (and hopefully also model) is that progressive church has only just barely been tried. We're still feeling our way. But I should also add, it *is* being tried, it's an actual real thing, and a book telling the story of that reality has value in and of itself.

These occasional pieces have been written while engaged in the actual, daily practice of progressive church. In this sense, they emerge out of specific experiences. What that means can vary widely from week-to-week. It might mean hosting safe space for those healing from religious trauma. It might mean partnering with area organizations during a pandemic to support the local Marshallese community. It might mean starting shelter and housing organizations or launching refugee resettlement efforts in the state. It might mean public advocacy at municipal meetings or quiet presence with queer kids impacted by hateful state laws. Or it might mean all the many typical activities most of us have experienced at church: worship, prayer, care, study, mutual aid. I hope this emergent, occasional approach has a reality solidifying effect, indicating there is a "there" there—actual church believing and ministering in these particular ways.

We should probably also say something briefly about this word "progressive." Progressivism arose in the North American context especially at the end of the 19th century, continuing up until the 1st World War, and focused on social activism and political reforms. It was not at that time tied to the same political parties to which it is tethered today (one famous progressive, Fighting Bob LaFollette, was for most of his life a Republican and then founded the Progressive Party in order to run for president... then he lost and the party collapsed).

When I use progressive in this book, I am not precisely referring to this historical progressivism, even though my use of the term resonates with many of the themes of the progressivism of that era—social justice, women's suffrage, government regulations and services providing social protections to improve the common good. Progressive church identifies with many of these "Leftist" values. But what progressive church signifies is the practice of church that arises out of the theological insights of the abolition movement, the social gospel, liberation theology, and other religious movements that provided the radical, prophetic energy for progressive politics.

Progressive Christians prioritize social justice as a form of neighbor love, understand care for the poor and the planet as central to Christian practice, resist co-optations of the Christian message that lead to xenophobia, homophobia, and other kinds of hate, and remain open to the insights of other religious traditions because of their relaxed approach to concerns about eternal salvation and greater focus on the common good here and now. They are shaped by and open to much of the analysis that has arisen out of critical theory, especially insights from workers, women, people of color, the poor, the LGBTQIA+ community, and indigenous peoples, that bring the experience of those at the intersections to bear on how we read Scripture, construct theology, and practice church. And admittedly, progressive Christianity is also defined by what it is not: it is *not* conservative evangelicalism.

A quick note on conservatives: I do not want to spend much time in this book defining or maligning conservatism, although given progressive resistance to much in conservatism it will come up. But I would like to offer a definition of what I believe conservatism is, so we aren't simply attacking a straw man. I take Wilhoit's law to be the most clear definition: "Conservatism consists of exactly one proposition, to wit: There must be in-groups whom the law protects but does not bind, alongside out-groups whom the law binds but does not protect." This law summarizes in one proposition much of what progressives oppose. One could say progressivism seeks legal protections for out-groups and a call to responsibility for in-groups to prioritize the needs of out-groups.

Periodically, people will point out that certain versions of progressive theology (and liberal theology) have, in the past, been complicit in harm. The most egregious example is liberal theology's co-optation by National Socialism in Germany under Hitler. However, I find this argument essentially incoherent when applied to 21st century progressivism. Many if not most of the theological commitments of liberal theologians in Germany leading up to the Second World War were not aligned with modern progressive Christianity and pre-date the generative impact 20th century liberation theologians have had on all our thinking. Additionally, progressive Christians have benefitted from the theological challenges raised by contemporary critics of liberal theology, Dietrich Bonhoeffer and Karl Barth in particular. Liberal theology enacted a way of thinking distanced from the person and work of Jesus Christ. In what follows in this book, you'll see I continuously tie progressive church practice to Jesus. He is our theological touchstone as moral exemplar and movement leader.

All of this to say: I take the warning seriously, that some of the risks involved in progressive Christianity need tending so as not to fall for siren songs, but the critical tools of the 20th century (beginning with the Frankfurt school but then continuing through many streams of thought) when applied creatively in conversation with progressive Christian theology, provide the equipment necessary to resist.

At this point the introduction has drifted from the practical messiness of composition and church life into more abstract realms of theory, and there's a time and place for that. But in this book, although we will sometimes dip our toes in those streams, we will keep the chapters focused and brief, occasional and messy. When appropriate, I'll suggest "for further reading" at the conclusion of a chapter. Most of the chapters in this book cover topics that deserve (and often have) many whole books written about them.

A Guidebook To Progressive Church proceeds through five sections. First, you receive an invitation. These short, sometimes quirky, chapters offer a few ways "in" to progressive church life and thought. Next, we examine some keywords in progressive church life—prayer, discipleship, pastor, Freidigkeit (a fancy German word for brazen freedom), and Jesus. Next, we include a series of chapters on beliefs, like atheism, the meaning of forgiveness, demythologization, ecumenical and interfaith work, the creed, salvation, and sacred texts. Then, because intersectionality plays such a central role in contemporary progressive Christian reflection, we look at topics of intersection like climate change, women's work, neurodiversity, queering, respectability, and Critical Race Theory. Finally, we include two sections, one on polis and one on praxis, the actual daily practice of progressive church and its impact on and relationship to the wider public political milieu or commons.

A few pointers on reading the book. I've attempted to organize it in such a way that it makes the most sense to read it straight through beginning to end. I've foregone footnotes and endnotes and kept any relevant notes embedded in the text itself in order to keep the reading experience more fluid and informal. Doing so will be an immersive experience. It's my hope, as much as possible, to convey what it's like to be part of a community that moves and thinks in these specific ways, unapologetically and somewhat against the odds. If you are not yet a part of a progressive community of faith, or do not live near one, it's my hope this can be an invitation to start one or move toward one. At the very least, it may provide some guidance on how to live your faith as a progressive in whatever context you find yourself.

But also, keep in mind that as heady as some of our most challenging theological or social issues may be, this is a guidebook to progressive *church*. I have quite intentionally kept the attention focused on how progressive Christian faith is lived out in local community. I invite all readers to always work to apply what you read here in the context of your own community life. Experience, after all, is a crucial loci in doing progressive theology. Your experiences, the work of your community, is the most important context for testing whether this guidebook "works."

PART I

INVITATION

1

WHY WE NEED A GUIDE TO PROGRESSIVE CHURCH

Adjectives are problematic. Although they help us know something is *that* sort of thing rather than *another* sort of thing, they also then invite us to believe or trust the way they modify by narrowing. Take as example the noun "church." We all have a rough semantic sense of what a "church" is. It's an assembly, a gathering of the faithful: in specifically Christian terms "the body of Christ." And it's also the word used to describe the building in which these kinds of assemblies gather, and from which such assemblies stage their neighbor-love in the world and their love of God in worship.

But once we start adding adjectives in front of that word "church," we begin to introduce complications. If you say you belong to a "Lutheran" church, this invokes an entire history of certain churches who are separated from or unique in comparison to other churches. We might say Lutheran churches are Protestant, or they are heirs of the Reformation, or they are a denomination in which certain gifts or charisms of the more general "church" are present. But then we'd also have to start asking which *kind* of Lutheran. Do we mean the more conservative Lutherans like Missouri synod, or the more liberal Lutherans like the ELCA? What does "Lutheran" even mean?

This is how the adjective becomes problematic. It can only carry a certain amount of meaning and beyond that each adjective can be broken. It can mean mutually contradictory things for which additional adjectives will be required.

Let's take the word "progressive." Is it increasingly an adjective for your kind of church? This isn't to say that the church you're a part of isn't also "Lutheran" or "Protestant" or "Christian." It's all of those things in various ways. But for the sake of this book, let's imagine the best one word to describe your church is "progressive," even if that adjective is ... problematic.

So what is a progressive church? A progressive church is like an iceberg. There's the part above the water you can see. There's also the larger portion below the water that floats the rest. The visible part of almost any progressive church focuses on LGBTQIA+ inclusion. This is essentially the litmus test for everything else, a synecdoche for the whole. Progressive churches are likely to have well-placed rainbow flags on banners all over. Those joining the church prioritize LGBTQIA+ inclusion in their selection process as they choose a church. These are the churches LGBTQIA+ Christians previously excluded from religious community find their way back to (those who desire to do so, that is). And progressive churches are still really the only churches anywhere who overtly welcome LGBTQIA+ people not just as members but also as pastors and leaders and teachers.

A few other social values circle around or near this LGBTQIA+ tip of the iceberg. In addition to inclusion, progressive churches are most likely among all liberal churches to align with the political Left, which is of course why some other Christians find them deeply problematic and (ahem) political. Because the wider culture assumes that Christians are conservative, any church that aligns with even some of the social or political values of the Left is going to be perceived as hyper-political simply because they break the *gestalt*.

If you are moderately aware of the top priorities of the Left today, you can imagine progressive churches sharing commitment with them on the following: anti-racism work, some kind of economic safety net for everyone (socialism), environmental advocacy, women in leadership, diversity and inclusion, and worker justice. Progressive Christianity shares many values with … the Left.

You might ask: Why? And isn't that the co-optation of the church by the values of the world?

Here's where we can really hone in on what it means to be a "progressive" Christian. We call ourselves progressive Christians, and organize progressive church, because some parts of our shared life together in Western culture in the 21st century arise very naturally out of the gospel of Jesus Christ as it has been communicated through Scripture and the history of Christian life. The gospel is "Left-resonant."

Rather than thinking of socialism as "worldly," as an outside force that is impinging on a supposedly co-opted pure "Christian worldview," the first step in understanding the underpinnings of progressive Christianity is to accept that every set of beliefs has a history and has been formed by many forces. There is no "pure" Christianity. All Christianities have a social location.

When many forms of conservative Christianity attempt to critique progressive Christianity as drawing too close to the culture, the main problem with such a critique is the failure of those conservative Christians to recognize the ways in which they are also shaped by the culture—just other aspects of it, or the same aspects of it under a different guise.

Progressive Christianity may be unique only in this way (and here we are going to the portion of the iceberg below the surface of the water) that it is willing to recognize and own, or at least continually strive to recognize and own, that faithfulness is continually a work in progress. And progressive church will live according to this admission, continually bringing the marks that center it (Scripture, tradition, etc.) into conversation with the experience and lives of those practicing it.

In other words, progressive church is about "progress," but not necessarily in the sense that it believes in continual advancement or ascent, but rather as movement toward. This is what makes it essentially different from conservatism, which has as its impulse to conserve a heritage it often then stewards with self-deceiving in-group exclusive nostalgia. Progressive Christianity recognizes it is likely we have gotten things wrong, that we continually get things wrong, that it is the work of the church to critically review its own way of being in the world and then strive to do better.

Today we find vast swathes of Christians in the United States rejecting critical-race theory, a secular movement that really ought to be, if considered, fully aligned with authentic Christianity. Critical-race theory is, at root, simply a tool in academic life to pry open past practice and examine how those practices have been shaped by race and ethnicity. It's like a secular parallel to the confession of sin.

Yet somehow conservative Christians find critical-race theory alarming. It's as if they fear a clear-eyed examination of all our various complicities in systemic injustice. Admittedly, progressive Christians themselves may find the application of critical-race theory discomfiting, because we come to a greater realization of our own complicity in racism in the course of its application. And then because we are discomfited, we may (unconsciously or implicitly) access some of the strategies we can muster, out of our own fragility, to resist the application of critical-race theory (CRT).

But what we won't do as progressive Christians is cease attempting to make progress on self-work and community work that can improve the lives of our neighbors, work that can make us more faithful Christians. This is why anti-racism work is work. It's an ongoing iterative process not of self-hate but of repentance. Critical-race theory is one such tool for that work.

Thus far I've been addressing you, the reader, as if we are a part of the same church. It's worth asking as we begin: Is this a guidebook "for" or "to" progressive church? If we say it is "for" progressive church, it low-key implies I've already figured out how to do and be progressive church and I'm giving readers a tour of something that already exists.

On the other hand, if we say it is "to" progressive church, it implies instead that progressive church is something we are all continually on our way toward. What I write here serves as a way-post or a sign for all those on the journey toward progressive church. For this reason, although I do value describing for readers the aspects of progressive church we already practice, I think it is more faithful and radically honest to admit that even those of us who inhabit progressive church space are still just figuring out what it is we're even doing, and continually reforming and growing out of the interaction between the faith we hold and the experiences we continue having. So, this is a guidebook "to" progressive church, and "we" are on the way toward it together.

This invites two more simple insights about "progressive" church by way of introduction, topics we will return to in more detail. The first is the influence of liberation theology on progressive church practice. Even if many progressive churches are not engaged in liberative practices as profound as liberation theology invites, they nevertheless live sympathetic to the insights of liberation theology. In their preaching and teaching they prioritize a "preferential option for the poor" (a framing first brought to wider attention by theologian Gustavo Guttierez). "The poor" in liberation theology are both literal and figurative. "The poor" can include different groups in different contexts. In a state passing anti-trans laws denying health care to trans youth, the poor are trans youth. In places where the police oppress and harm African-Americans, the poor are Black lives. Etc. The point in all of it is that church from a liberation theology perspective prioritizes the lived experience of "the poor" and confesses that the gospel is either living and active or not if it offers a freeing and healing word specifically for "the poor."

This focus on "the poor" is not to the exclusion of the kinds of hopes prevalent in wider Christian culture (which I think centers around getting "saved") but is rather the neighbor-love corollary. That is to say, it makes very little sense to prioritize or hyper-focus on an other-worldly salvation if in the meantime our poor neighbors are being left behind in the present. If you can imagine a form of salvation that offers you eternal life in Jesus when you die but brush aside prioritizing real life for all our neighbors (and the planet) in the present, there is something inherently problematic with your soteriology.

The second point is more meta: One reason progressive

church is still an unknown in many Christian contexts and unfamiliar to the wider culture is because it has been, to date, rarely tried. Many moderate and liberal churches certainly gesture at things like LGBTQIA+ inclusion. Far fewer actually practice it. As we often discuss in our church, there is a massive difference between saying to LGBTQIA+ Christians that they are welcome to come to "our" church, vs. saying together with LGBTQIA+ Christians in our community, "We've designed this queer space especially with you in mind." Sometimes we have tried, and even succeeded, and in this book I'll also be boasting about these successful attempts. It's worth showing it can be done.

Progressive churches are often asked: *Why is your church committed to LGBTQIA+ inclusion?* The best answer to this question is likely another question, *Why aren't all churches?* It is exhausting trying to rationalize something so self-evident. Presumably those asking this question have been in contexts where it is self-evident Christians should exclude queer people. By acquiescing and answering the question as proposed, we've failed even before starting because we concede the point that the case even needs to be made for inclusion. But the reverse is more true: exclusionary churches should have to make the case for their exclusions. Ask: *Why is bigotry a part of your faith?*

Why aren't all the inclusive Christians currently attending non-progressive churches not asking themselves and their leadership THAT question? This is the kind of question a progressive church tends to ask, and why we need a guidebook to progressive church. Given how many books have been written *against* progressive Christianity, it's time to turn the tables and place reverse pressure on the haters. Proudly stating who we are and steadfastly reversing the pressure is an essential move.

FOR FURTHER READING

G. Gutierrez, *A Theology of Liberation: History, Politics, Salvation*, Orbis Books, 1988.

2

SO YOU MIGHT VISIT A PROGRESSIVE CHURCH?

Most Sundays I go to church because it's my job. On those five or six Sundays a year when I'm out of town for work or travel, I find myself in the same situation as many others, asking myself whether I should go to church, and where.

Most often I do this alone. My family typically doesn't consider church attendance a vacation activity. I'm kind of the opposite: not only do I love to go to church because of what it means, I also love what it teaches me about the communities I'm in.

Some of the more memorable church services I've visited over the last decade include: a ski hill chapel at Copper Mountain, Colorado; a Vietnamese congregation in Des Moines, Iowa; a Roman Catholic parish near the North Shore in Hawaii; an historic UCC church in Camden, Maine; an African Methodist Episcopal church in DC; multi-day worship at our denominational World Hunger Gathering in Houston; an Eastern Orthodox service in St Paul, Minnesota; a Hussite Church in Prague; Marshallese Arkansas United Church of Christ in Springdale, Arkansas; an Old Catholic Parish in Pasadena, California; an Episcopal Church in St. Louis, Missouri.

When I seek out these churches I follow a few steps. Sometimes I simply try to find the church closest to me. In Camden and St. Louis the churches were literally right across the street. I highly recommend at least scoping out the church in closest proximity to you.

If I can I also try to find churches that are LGBTQIA+ affirming. Increasingly I'm not much convinced I want to worship in a place that isn't committed clearly to full inclusion, even if it is conveniently located.

Although I recognize visiting a church on vacation is not the same as visiting a church in order to consider joining it, I have discovered a couple of postures toward worship visitation that may be useful for anyone out there considering a church.

The first is curiosity. It's valuable to attend church wearing an amateur sociologist or liturgist or historian hat. If nothing else you leave having learned something, and such a posture has a way of modifying any experiences that might otherwise seem negative.

The second is intentional strangeness. For this reason, I especially recommend attending churches conducting service in a language not your own. Often the best church experience is in a language I don't speak, because it's rare in other contexts to be able to listen to and try out another tongue, and because it significantly broadens who we assume God to be when that God is spoken to in a language we don't comprehend.

The third is personal piety. If I know I'm there for the communion meal, or to hear a word in the sermon, or to pray with intentionality, or for the chance to sing with gusto, then it's what I bring to it that matters most.

The fourth is like curiosity, but I guess I'd call it parallelism. When we travel, we often decide to take in local concerts, or visit museums, or try restaurants. What is wrong with also including worship as something we do to take in the sights and sounds of a place? And whether it's a chance to hear the local dialect, see the architecture, or pick up on a sense of the place, a worship service is a particularly rich way to do so no matter how you look at it.

I think this is longform encouragement to all you reading to worship when you travel, but also an invitation to progressive church if you've never tried it, because you might find out there's been another country right near you this whole time. That's often something I learn when I visit a church. It reveals a whole territory.

Over two decades of ministry I've heard many stories of how people end up at progressive church. Most often people arrive because they sought an inclusive church that matched their values and where they could be themselves. They were seeking a place where questions were welcome and they felt safe.

But the journey to getting there was often emotionally and relationally complicated. In some cases it meant ending relationships, overcoming fears, addressing trauma.

For many the prospect of visiting (sometimes even considering) a new church or shifting from one church to another is incredibly fraught. It is astounding to listen to descriptions of what it is like to leave church, live in exile from church, or return to church. Life in religious community is often closely connected to our sense of self, and so moving between traditions can be an existential journey.

Since this is a guidebook to progressive church, we should take time to consider these existential realities. Let's say you are currently not a member of a progressive church but you are curious or considering. The journey to such a church will look very different depending on your starting point.

For some this journey is geographical. Those living in remote or more conservative parts of the country may not even have a progressive church somewhere near them to join. In this case the complications are logistical.

For others the journey is religious. The tradition in which they were raised taught certain basic assumptions, truths, postures of belief, and the journey includes deciding what of all that can be released, what can be retained, what surfaces as they begin to move toward something new.

For others the difficulty may be the reality of joining any kind of organization at all. There may be social anxieties around a first visit, a multitude of questions about how to appropriately attend (how to act, how to dress, how to make eye contact, how to smile), as well as the very real question of whether they want to commit, or commit again, to a specific community of people.

The stories I have heard of this journey have been many and varied. Some of our people have come from closed communities like Jehovah's Witness. Others come from very strict backgrounds like Church of Christ or Southern Baptist. Still others are returning after long absence from church (they left or were kicked out or simply drifted away). Others are brand new to church, seeking out for the first time a community of faith that aligns with their values and emerging beliefs.

For some, part of the journey is processing religious trauma. Some find that returning to safe and inclusive space is part of their healing. For others the journey is simply strange, mystical even, because church is strange, especially if it has not been part of your longstanding habit. At church we do things like hand people bread, tell them it is the body of Christ, and invite them to eat it... as if this were entirely normal.

So let's say you have picked up this book and find yourself in one of these descriptions: you're ready to at least consider progressive church. Some parts seem daunting, others invigorating, some confusing, some clear. But you are ready.

Here's a set of steps I hope will help.

- Be kind to yourself. It's not easy to leave a community, especially if there are strong family ties.

Not everyone can leave, at least not literally, or not right away.

- Let this book and other resources be your friend. There are great web sites and communities online, from Reddit threads to YouTube channels to Facebook groups. You are not alone in taking such steps.

- Many progressive churches livestream services. This can be a low-key way to try out a new community. For those whose barrier is geographic this may be the only way to connect.

- If you have decided to visit a progressive church, there are certain markers you can use to trust there won't be a bait and switch. The Reconciling in Christ badge (our denominational indicator of being an inclusive church), or a listing at gaychurch.org

- If part of your journey is religious trauma, even entering the church building itself will be strange. You may find yourself driving through the parking lot but not walking in. Once inside remember the body keeps the score. Sometimes even the simplest parts of church can bring back memories, create a sense of dissociation, trigger reactions. So be kind to yourself.

- So often people have been trained that doubts or questions are a barrier to faith, as if you cannot belong if you don't believe all the right things before you arrive. Progressive church is especially different in this way, we really believe the doubts and questions are a part of faith itself, they aren't in the way, they are the way.

- There will likely be surprises as you observe what is identified as sin in progressive churches. Rather than personal sins leading to damnation, progressives tend to focus on systemic sins that create oppression. This can be a relief. It can also be challenging, inasmuch as when you arrived and sought refuge you were then immediately invited to join the fight. But that's ok. Taking up the cross which is what Christians are called to do can be passed around, taken up at different times, in an ebb and flow of rest and activity.

- Find your people.

- Because progressives tend not to implement strong authoritarian patterns, it's unlikely you'll be told what to do. This is a good thing except in one way: the community will wait for you to take the initiative. You get to define how you engage, which requires being proactive.

Few progressive churches have had the opportunity to start from a blank slate. Most have a history. Visitors and inquirers will observe marks of this history in their form of worship, the build of their church, where they get their pastors. It's a good reminder that almost no community is a community without a history, the wrinkles around the eyes that tell the story of time and experience. I mention this as an insight, not one of the steps per se but simply a tool for those visiting churches: some things you'll experience in almost any church are just part of the furniture, and sometimes the furniture has gotten old.

I started this chapter with a personal testimony of church visitation, then shifted to a gentle list of steps for visiting a progressive church. In this last section, I'm going for a more combative approach. Fair warning.

There's a logical fallacy I reflect on often: *abusus non tollit proprium usus.* "The abuse of something does not disallow its appropriate use." This means even if (many) churches abusively wed Christianity to nationalism and racism, Christianity as a whole is not therefore invalidated.

Why would we allow abusers to steal something from us? I'm assuming there's something about Christianity, progressive Christianity in general, that draws and attracts you. Just because conservative Christians *believe* they have the market cornered on Christianity doesn't mean they actually do.

I'm not willing to allow conservative abuse of Christianity to define Christianity. I love Jesus too much, I believe in the potential organizing capacity of Christian community, I have witnessed over the years the depth of positive impact Christianity rightly ordered can have, I trust the testimony of faithful Christians over many centuries. I love the beauty of liturgy, I adore church buildings, my dearest friendships and relationships are in religious spaces.

I love the church. I'm not going to allow anyone to steal this joy from me. So partially, if you're considering visiting a progressive church, you might think of it as an act of joyful resistance. Go to church to "stick it to the man." Go to church to take back the joy. Make the choice on your own terms, not the terms set by the abusers.

FOR FURTHER READING

R.H. Evans, *Searching for Sunday: Loving, Leaving, And Finding the Church*, Thomas Nelson, 2015

3

WHY A TAROT CARD TABLE AT CHURCH AT A QUEER-FRIENDLY HALLOWEEN PARTY IS THE MOST CHRISTIAN THING EVER

For the past couple of years our church has hosted Queer Camp, a summer camp experience for LGBTQIA+ youth. During the school year, we also put on mini-camp events to maintain connections between the campers. It's always like a big reunion whenever we gather. One of the biggest events is our Halloween party, which we humorously call *The Nightmare Before Gay Christmas*.

Our general approach to organizing events at the intersection of community and church life is to host space and allow whatever happens at the event to be shaped by how the community shares their gifts. For the Halloween party we invited participants to "table." Some of our LGBTQIA+ partners set up tables with stickers and candy and some artists offered facepainting and other Halloween-themed activities. Plus lots of sugar.

We really have a blast. The kids wear amazing costumes. This year we busted out not just one, but two smoke machines and we even had a cauldron with dry ice.

But the highlight of the evening was the quiet serenity of a tarot-reading station in the back room. It was a space of calm and healing and joy.

If you're unfamiliar with tarot cards, perhaps everything I'm going to write from here on out will be particularly helpful. Regardless of your current relationship with "pagan" practices, I'm inviting you for this moment to consider them with an open mind, because if I do this well I'm probably describing the beating heart of what I love about progressive Christianity.

Okay, so I first need to admit that I don't use tarot cards myself. In fact, I don't intentionally practice any traditions outside of the Christianity in which I've been raised. I'm not a multiple religious practitioner of any sort, at least not on purpose. I do recognize that what I think of as Christianity has always without exception been the weaving together of various spiritualities, from Judaism to Greek philosophy to Zoroastrianism to capitalism. There is no pure Christianity apart from its relating to other traditions.

My second admission: I have always assumed that tarot card reading was a kind of spirituality related to the occult. But in writing this post, I've discovered that isn't so.

Tarot, intriguingly, though mostly found in the New Age section of the bookstore, originated in the 15th century in Europe as a card game. *It started out as a game, and can still be used in this way.* It was a few centuries later, in the 18th century, that some French mystics began introducing the use of the cards for divination purposes (and paired it with a fabrication that it had origins in Egypt). For a few centuries there was a decline in their use, but in the same way we have seen a more general resurgence of board games and gaming, tarot cards have made a comeback.

When a local psychic and tarot card reader (and parent of a camper) offers to host a card-reading table, my go-to response is, "Yes please!" And perhaps this is my first point. As a progressive Christian I do not have an immediate visceral negative reaction to the spiritual practices arising in the culture around me. Instead, I initially approach the spiritual practices of others with a level of phenomenological curiosity (it clearly makes sense to you, so I'll listen to you and what it means to you) and second with the simple understanding that all of us are multiple religious practitioners.

In attempting to do some of my own ancestor work, I would add: tarot cards are a part of my own ethnic heritage. They arose in Europe and remained popular in Germany and other places at a moment in time concurrent with the impact of the Reformation on Christian life in that region. Which is to say, to have tarot cards at a church is not a complete novum. They aren't even "foreign." They come from where I come from, where our religious tradition comes from geographically.

Doing this kind of historical work is important. It's important to learn, for example, that even a Lutheran like Phillip Melanchthon (close partner of Martin Luther in writing our confessional documents) was also considered the "astrologer of the Reformation" because he considered astrology an "art of dignity" and defended it on Christian grounds. He even published an entire essay in 1535 on this topic, *The Dignity of Astrology*.

We all have some retrieval work to do to continually come to greater awareness of how much more complex the origins are of our religious traditions.

I was recently clued into this insight when I picked up *Post-Colonial Astrology: Reading the Planets through Capital, Power, and Labor* by Alice Sparkly Kat. Post-colonial reflections are an integral part of the academic life of almost all progressive theology, and such tools have been applied to salutary effect in ecclesiology and theology the last couple of decades. I still remember reading Edward Said's *Orientalism* in seminary and being forever changed by it. The whole notion that we construct our sense of "others" in order to construct who "we" are.

Anyway, as I read *Post-Colonial Astrology* I watched a nimble thinker apply some of the same tools to their own astrological practices, and had a small moment of revelation: We're in this together, aren't we? Which is to say, even if I did decide to connect intentionally to astrology (I don't currently), a progressive astrologer would have a lot of questions, ways of interrogating the work of astrology itself. None of us can run off to other spiritual traditions and discover ones that are pure and good, unsullied by the world.

Returning to the tarot card table at the Halloween party: many if not most LGBTQIA+ youth have experienced religious trauma if they have been affiliated with Christian churches. The work of the church in relationship to queer youth, therefore, must take account of this. We perpetuate the trauma if we try to invite youth back into contexts or spiritual practices they have experienced as harmful.

This is where the sheer presence of the tarot card table becomes powerful. Many queer people still wish to access spiritual practices, and one of the gentler modes for this are things like paganism, or tarot cards, or astrology, along with other "New Age" spiritualities that are not as freighted with the weight of historic oppression of LGBTQIA+ people, and also are not part of the dominant culture. New Age is itself, in a sense, queer.

But just as queer people are not homogenous, neither is New Age spirituality. It is also not one monolithic thing. One person may be using tarot cards just as a game. Another may actually be attempting cartomancy. One astrologer may be making literal predictions based on the planets. Another may think of it as an exercise of the imagination. Practice ranges widely.

Talk with practitioners, and you discover they reject, together with critics, some of the same parts of what is erroneously all lumped together as "the occult." The night of the party, I spent some time talking with a friend who identifies as a pagan, and we both agreed we do not like Ouija boards, because summoning spirits is very different (and lacks the consent of the summoned spirit?) from other spiritual practices that double as games. It's an easy error to make, but an error nonetheless, to gather everything up into one basket and then ascribe guilt by association. But if this is something that frustrates us about the frequent rejection of Christianity, it should also frustrate us about our own outsider perspective of New Age practices, right?

Circling back a final time to that tarot card table. *What do you think it feels like for a queer youth to come to a queer-friendly Halloween party at a church, then sit down with a friendly tarot card reader and read the cards together?*

This is not a question, an interaction, I would have imagined a decade ago, and yet I'm so here for it.

What I observe is an overall relaxing, a lowering of the guards. Kind of like, "Oh, ok, I can be here as my authentic queer self and that's okay, and this place is also safe for this tarot card reader who is donating her time. Yes maybe there's some Jesus water over there in the sanctuary I can joke about, but nobody here seems to have any anxiety about me getting baptized or saved or about getting me to believe any particular thing about any of it. So I'll sit down here, because cards are fun, and because I'd like to do a bit more self-reflection through some guided imagery and conversation. I'll bracket for the time-being that this even is a church building. Ah yes, I can actually play here."

The other change that happens through this kind of openness to the other: the exercise of the fulness of their spiritual practice becomes a deepening of my own faith. I honestly hadn't been aware that tarot cards were first and foremost (and still are) primarily a game. I love games. So at a baseline secular level I simply know more. This opens my curiosity.

Additionally, it turns out we're not even alone in exploring the synergy between Tarot and Christianity. There's a recent book out, *The Contemplative Tarot: A Christian Guide to the Cards,* which I would never have known about except in order to write this chapter I googled "Tarot" and "Christianity."

The Religion News Service in an interview asks the author: **"What are some of the different ways one can use the cards? You use them in prayer, which may be a little different than how others might think of using them."**

She replies:

There's been sort of a revival of tarot just in general in the last five or 10 years, and it's been really interesting to see the different ways people use tarot now. Even the non-Christians I know who use tarot rarely use it for any sort of divination. Most people I know who read tarot now, even people who are not Christian, use it as a tool for self-reflection. I would liken it more to therapy than fortunetelling.

That's very similar to the way that I use tarot. I liken it to Visio Divina, a contemplative prayer practice that translates to "divine seeing." It involves praying with images — to look at an image, to insert yourself into the image, to spend time with an image in contemplation and to see if God is speaking to you in some way through the image.

That's lovely, right? So much of conservative Christianity has mystified and "othered" spiritual practices not included in the narrow band of what is allowed in evangelical churches it takes a winsome champion like Brittany Muller to draw us back into how everyday and creative something like image-bearing cards can be to enliven the human spirit. Remaining open and curious is modeled here, illustrating how a progressive church perspective prioritizes care and love, watching for how it is practiced in various traditions, then adopting or adapting as needed.

FOR FURTHER READING

B. Muller, *The Contemplative Tarot: A Christian Guide to the Cards,* Essentials, 2022.

4

TEN (UNCOMFORTABLE) STEPS
YOU CAN TAKE RIGHT NOW

A recent college graduate and early reader of this guidebook recommended a list of steps anyone can take right now to connect with progressive church. In particular she recommended a list of the uncomfortable things progressive churches can and should encourage their members to do in daily life. We emphasize "uncomfortable" steps precisely because, although conservative Christians often accuse progressive Christianity of "conforming" to the spirit of this world, in reality many of the commitments of progressive Christianity are profoundly counter-cultural.

My first recommendation is a typical one for a pastor, I guess, but I really do believe in it. *Commit to gathering weekly with a community.* There are many reasons to gather weekly and mostly they are not related to counting butts in pews. Gathering weekly is something almost all social organizations recognize as valuable for cohesion and movement building. Rotary clubs meet weekly. Alcoholics Anonymous meets weekly. Many people go to a therapist weekly. Dungeons and Dragons groups meet weekly. Weekly is just enough to build relationships, offer care, build networks, while not so frequent as to over-burden. Commit to weekly and over time you'll be surprised what grows, what shifts, in your relationship with the community. Not to mention, attending weekly means weekly hearing Scripture, singing progressive hymns, attending to a sermon, praying for a just world, all central to progressive Christian values.

Second, I recommend you *think about your participation in a progressive church less in terms of what you get out of it and more what you put into it.* Yes, weekly worship can be a therapeutic realignment, an energy boost for the week. But if you go to church on Sunday remembering to place food in the Little Free Pantry, watch for the lonely person in a pew who may need a caring conversation, and open to one challenge shifting your life more toward care of creation and love of neighbor, this will have a dramatic impact on your life, and especially over time.

Third, I recommend you *wear weird shirts or hats. And fly flags.* Admittedly, this is a stereotype. Progressive t-shirt shops like Raygun have become tremendously popular combining progressive politics with humor and regional themes, and indeed progressives do fly flags (the Pride flag in particular, the up-to-date version of which is actually called the "progress" flag). But there's a reason signs and shirts matter; they signal. I know older members of our church who always wear Pride buttons or pins precisely because they came out as older adults and wish there had been more signals around them indicating who was safe, and what spaces were safe. Being out and proud and loud is tremendously important in a cultural context and historical moment when simply the right to exist is being challenged by state governments and big churches.

Fourth, *pick one climate change action you can take and stick to it, long-term.* When Greta Thunberg began her climate strikes in Sweden, she was a lone student on the street. It took time for people to join her, and it was her persistence and focus that had (and has) the greatest impact. Often we become overwhelmed considering massive life-change, and given how impactful climate change is on the world, we are tempted to think the only response is to change everything. But in reality beginning somewhere, with one action, can move mountains. Pick something, preferably something public or communal that invites others to change as well, and then keep doing it.

Fifth, *read theology.* Again, this does indeed sound like the kind of recommendation a pastor would make, but I really mean it. I've ended up pastoring a progressive church and writing a guidebook to progressive church in large part through wide and steady life-long reading, theology in particular. It's theology that to a considerable degree got us into our present troubles, and so it will be careful theological work that will also get us out of it. Much of popular evangelical theology makes it to the top of the bestseller list and ends up widely read, discussed, and shared. An important form of counterbalance to this is to read otherwise. I've recommended a book at the end of each chapter in this guidebook, and if you read those, most of them contain additional bibliographies and footnotes. Use those as a guide for continued reading.

Sixth, *create*. As just one example of what progressive church needs, we need a much bigger songbook. We need hymns to sing our faith in worship. We need art for our worship spaces, images for our protest signs, poetry for our meditation, novels to imagine other worlds, podcasts to know we're not alone, cartoons to make us laugh and tell the truth.

Seventh, *be a friend*. If you feel alone or geographically distant from progressive church, make use of social media networks to connect. If you are already a part of a progressive church, trust that one of the most powerful practices you can engage is befriending. In many parts of the country (and the world) progressives feel embattled, over-whelmed, and exhausted. Even if you don't have the bluster to speak out at town hall, nevertheless you can befriend someone who does. Also, befriending includes being a friend of the organizations doing the work. Research what organizations in your community are truly forwarding progressive causes, aligned with Christian progressive values, and support them, show up with them, be their champion.

Eighth, *give money*. Not everyone is in a position to do this, but many are. If you feel busy with family life and work but want to make sure progressive institutions like the church thrive, giving them financial support is probably *the* most effective single action you can take. Your donations pay salaries, keep the building repaired, and go through the door to those in need.

Ninth, *do the work*. Progressives invite themselves, as part of their Christian practice, to repent, as do most Christians, but progressives in particular understand that repentance is aligned with the work to which progressive movements call us. Do anti-racism work. Examine your privilege. Struggle with the ways implicit bias has influenced your perspectives on gender and sexuality. Consider reparations. All of these are truly progressive causes that, when considered in light of Christian theology, are also truly the work Christians are called to by the gospel of Jesus Christ.

Finally, *nap*. Given that progressivism is such a posture of struggle, it's crucial to keep in mind rest is an aspect of the work, not an escape from it. As The Nap Ministry proclaims, "Rest is resistance." While you're at it, maybe join Bernie Sanders in his campaign for a 32-hour work week, and campaign for a universal basic income for everyone?

FOR FURTHER READING

T. Hersey, *Rest Is Resistance: A Manifesto*, Little, Brown Spark, 2022.

5

AMONG THE PROGRESSIVES

Progressive Christianity is far from uni-vocal, and there is some value in naming the progressive voices among whom this guidebook situates itself. Even if the practice of progressive church is largely grassroots, often quieter and far more mundane than many of the NY Times bestselling authors included here, nevertheless many of these popular voices serve as important touch-points helping us locate ourselves within the "field" of progressive Christianity.

I will not go into detail about individual authors, because in many instances whole chapters or books could be written about each of them. Instead, I'm going to organize authors (yes, they're all authors) into a variety of groupings. Think of this as a sampling, an admittedly non-exhaustive catalog of progressives (I'm anxious because I'm sure I'll omit someone others believe shouldn't be omitted), designed to be useful both for situating this book among these other voices and as a recommended reading list for the curious.

Some of the most famous progressives are Roman Catholic. Chief among these include the prolific contemplative writer Richard Rohr, the winsome LGBTQIA+ theologian James Alison, the martyr Archbishop Romero (of blessed memory), and the world-famous musician Sinéad O'Connor. Progressive Catholics gather a large readership and bleed over into traditional Roman Catholic spaces in sometimes intriguing ways because even the core of Roman Catholicism is, on many social justice issues, aligned with progressive Christianity.

Another very prominent group of progressives are evangelicals, most of whom have moved out of or on from evangelicalism. Included here would be President Jimmy Carter, who almost more than anyone else embodies in his life and actions what progressive Christianity professes; the quite popular author and creative Rob Bell, biblical interpreter Pete Enns, widely read blogger John Pavlovitz, country rock star Dolly Parton, *Sojourners'* magazine founder Jim Wallis, memoirist Rachel Held Evans (of blessed memory), Tripp Fuller host of Homebrewed Christianity podcast, and emergent Christianity leader Brian McClaren. Evangelicals who move toward progressivism often must undertake an actual exodus but can at least sometimes still tap into the cultural dominance of evangelicalism to reach a wide audience.

More native to progressive Christianity are the Mainliners, including my own denomination's rock star Nadia Bolz-Weber, but also Bishop Michael Curry of the Episcopal church,

Pulitzer-prize winning novelist Marilynne Robinson, practical theologian and historian Dorothy Bass, and the editor of *The Christian Century*, Peter Marty. For the most part (with the notable exception of Nadia Bolz-Weber) mainline Protestants gather the attention of a less sizeable portion of the total Christian audience in North America, but nevertheless are a mainstay of the Christian move toward increasingly progressive Christian values.

Black progressives are also prominent in the overall movement, with representation like the philosopher Cornel West, the leader of the renewed Poor Peoples' Campaign William Barber II, and the best-selling devotional author of *Black Liturgies*, Cole Arthur Riley. If any one person can be said to be carrying the mantel of progressive Christianity today, it is William Barber II, currently now Founding Director of the Center for Public Theology and Public Policy at Yale Divinity School, President and Senior Lecturer of Repairers of the Breach, Co-Chair of the Poor People's Campaign: A National Call For Moral Revival, and a bishop with The Fellowship of Affirming Ministries. In many ways the Black progressive movement has carried the torch of progressive Christianity more than any other community.

We cannot overlook the "peace" church movement when we speak of progressive Christianity. Popular voices here include Shane Claiborne, and Melissa Florer-Bixler. Although peace churches may diverge from progressives on some issues, and in this way are like progressive Catholics, nevertheless they serve as important voices in the overall progressive Christian tradition. They push progressives to wrestle even more intentionally with issues like the death penalty and war.

My own pantheon of progressive Christians, the ones who have most directly influenced my own work as a pastor and theologian, do not all come from North America, and far less are living. I include at least the Communist priest Alan Ecclestone, the feminist German theologian Dorothee Soelle, the martyr Dietrich Bonhoeffer (of blessed memory), New Testament scholar Ernst Käsemann, process theologian Catherine Keller, Wil Gafney creator of the Women's Lectionary, interfaith religious scholar John Thatamanil, and the historian of liberal and progressive Christianity, Gary Dorrien. There are many, many others, but these are especially influential in my thinking.

Finally, I might mention some of the prominent voices within my own denomination, the Evangelical Lutheran Church in America. Lutherans who have in the last five years published wonderfully insightful works at the intersection of progressive Christianity include: Elle Dowd, Heidi Neumark, Emily M.D. Scott, Angela Denker, Lenny Duncan, Ross Murray, and Jamie Bruesehoff.

If progressive Christianity is relatively new to you (or honestly even if it isn't) I recommend an entirely pleasurable assignment: create a reading list from just some of these authors. Not only would it serve as a deeper introduction to progressive Christianity for those who are new to progressive church, it also would serve as an excellent conversation partner for active progressive Christians.

At the beginning of this chapter, I emphasized these were almost all authors, and I raise this as an issue because, in some instances, the fact that we primarily encounter progressive Christianity in texts rather than in church life may distort our perceptions, giving the impression only authors (or primarily authors) can be truly progressive. The reality is more mundane, there are little progressive churches peppering the whole country, in every state, in many cities, with progressive nuns at picket lines and progressive church communities going about the daily work of serving as the hands and feet of Jesus in community.

But in the mix, many of those listed above publish books as a by-product of what they do in community, and books are great because they are an available resource helping us see other communities of faith and test our practice of church over-against what they have written. Books may have their limits because they selectively tell the story from specific perspectives. This guidebook is no exception. It's quite idiosyncratically by a single author, emerging from one local practice of progressive church. But if you keep this in mind, that mine or anyone's voice is one voice, then even more reason to read around among the many authors I've mentioned, so that by the end of the journey you hear all of them as a resonant progressive choir.

PART II

KEYWORDS

6

WHAT, TO A PROGRESSIVE, IS PRAYER?

ord have mercy is my most frequent prayer. It's what I
pray when I don't know what else to say, when otherwise
my prayers would fall apart into incomprehensible groanings. In
the face of the tragic and incomprehensible, we offer what little
we have, which colloquially is often expressed as our "thoughts
and prayers." If thoughts and prayers are sacrilegiously coupled
with studied and intentional inaction, politicizing disregard for
human lives, it is no wonder the response from those grieving
and afraid is "don't give me your thoughts and prayers."

However, *abusus non tollit proprium usus*. The abuse of
something does not disallow its appropriate use. With prayer,
simply because we witness hypocritical prayers does not mean
prayer is unimportant or ineffective. Prayer is in fact the most
important thing, it is our manner of union with God, which
then moves us into action in the world aligned with God. Prayer

is in Christian perspective us joining Christ's prayers in the Spirit out of abiding love for God's world. Even the lament "don't give me your thoughts and prayers" is in fact a kind of prayer.

Let's take a real-world example: in the current back-and-forth on social media around gun control (we should ban AR-15s today) and our culture's continued hatemongering and loneliness generating, perhaps we lose sight of this theological insight, that much more is prayer than we realize. In our grief, in our rage, we may miss that even our own social media posts are themselves prayers.

The Cappadocian Gregory of Nyssa in a very early series of sermons wrote,

"Prayer is intimacy with God and contemplation (*theoria*) of the invisible. It satisfies our yearnings and makes us equal with angels. Through it good prospers, evil is destroyed, and sinners will be converted. Prayer is the enjoyment of things present and the substance of things to come... Now I think that, even if we spent our whole life in constant communion with God in prayer and thanksgiving, we should be as far from having made God an adequate return as if we had not even begun to desire making the Giver of all good things such a return." (Sermon 1; The Lord's Prayer, Beatitudes, 24-25).

So yes, tell it like it is, name the idolatrous prayers that the NRA and politicians backed by the NRA are praying. Those are prayers to their god Moloch and acknowledgement of their willingness to sacrifice people (especially children) at the altar of their god.

But then join Christ in his prayers which he continually brings before God his Father. Use all the prayers at your disposal. Pray the prayers of lament and rage in the Psalms. Pray prayers that good will prosper, that evil will be destroyed, that hard-hearted politicians will be converted, that violent young men considering hateful violence might turn toward peace and healing.

Pray all those prayers. **Then also, and importantly, act.** At the time of this writing you could do at least the following today: write your senators and advocate that they pass the Domestic Terrorism Prevention Act; support organizations who have been involved over the long haul in promoting gun sense and safety like Moms Demand Action; pray the Litany In The Wake Of A Mass Shooting or organize a group to pray it with you. You can also challenge bigoted religious communities who still exclude and condemn LGBTQIA+ people, even and especially your own communities. Do the work. Finally, stop voting into office craven politicians who sacrifice people at the altar of Moloch.

Yes, many in every generation have "sterilize[d] living religion into formula and ritual, where no psalm may be recited in a new form lest it perhaps turn into a genuine prayer" (Dorothee Soelle). But isn't it precisely our deepest hope that a genuine prayer would emerge? Because a genuine prayer would change everything.

∾

The most important work progressive Christians can engage in is public testimony related to the proper function and place of "public prayer" in our communities. I include here at the end a letter to the editor I sent off to our local newspaper in 2023 after I grew quite tired of attending public meetings at which the elected officials prayed constantly "in Jesus' name."

A Letter to the Editor re: Prayer at Public Meetings

I have long been opposed to Christian prayers at the opening of public meetings. I think the case is simply made that when the chair of a city council or quorum court or some other entity prays "in the name of Jesus" they violate the Establishment Clause. When such governing bodies make a habit of praying these sorts of prayers month after month and year after year, they violate the religious liberties of minority traditions our Founders sought to protect.

The United States has always been a nation of diverse religions. At its inception it wasn't even particularly religious, so the modern shift turning municipal meetings into mini revivals is especially untoward. Perhaps if a civic body planned over time to offer prayers or meditations representing the full range of religious traditions (and lack thereof) within its community, such practice might be equitable. But as it stands in most places it's just blatantly Christian nationalist.

The constitutional case against prayers at public meetings is clear, but perhaps Christians who inflict such prayers on those gathered might benefit from hearing a Christian case against such prayers.

This is an attempt at that.

Let's start with the times Jesus prays in his own name at government assemblies. Wait! Are you struggling to remember them? Well, that's because Jesus was rarely, if ever, found in the presence of the legal authorities.

However, there is one moment, a crucial moment. Jesus is brought before Pilate for a trial. Pilate asks Jesus, "Are you the king of the Jews?" Jesus enigmatically replies, "Is that your own idea?" Then Pilate accuses Jesus of being a king, and Jesus replies, "You say that I am a king. In fact, the reason I was born and came into the world is to testify to the truth. Everyone on the side of truth listens to me" (John 18:37 NIV).

In other words, Jesus when presented with an opportunity to pray to his Father, or to emphasize his own name and elevate it, instead shifts attention away from himself and toward ... the truth. Jesus is willing to find himself and be present exclusively in the truth, which intriguingly is a secular concept available to everyone in a democracy, regardless of their religion.

This shift in attention away from Jesus and toward the truth is of a piece with the theological motif found throughout the New Testament, the notion that God's power is made perfect in weakness (2 Corinthians 12:9), that Jesus "made himself nothing" (Philippians 2:7). Jesus is in, with and under the things of this world, and has no need to take pride of place or be named at the beginning of meetings. He lives the dictum encapsulated by the great Danish Christian educator Nikolai Grundtvig, "Human first, then Christian."

I'm reminded of a recent conversation. A retired judge in our community proudly told me he had prayed "in the name of Jesus" at a Rotary meeting. This made some of the other Rotarians uncomfortable, and his response to them was dramatic. "Don't you know I'm willing to die right now for Jesus?" He told me this story because he had just learned I was a pastor and thought I'd be proud of his actions.

I think this judge had an odd martyr complex, as if naming Jesus in a prayer at a Rotary meeting was the height of Christian heroism.

But when I heard this, I said, "If you're so willing to die, why don't you die to your own pride right now? If you are willing to die for the Lord who died for you, maybe join him in his own weakness and poverty and lack of self-assertion? Why not take up the cross of not inflicting your religious beliefs on others?"

Elected officials who pray at public meetings "in the name of Jesus" have convinced themselves they are being a witness to Jesus. It's embarrassingly performative and tremendously out of place. What they're really doing is witnessing to their own privilege and power, their "right" to inflict their religious views on others. Such a witness accomplishes the opposite of its supposed ends. It pushes hearers away from Jesus rather than drawing them close.

It lacks truth.

No one wants to draw close to a smug and self-satisfied

deity piously offered on the lips of smug and self-satisfied officials. The Jesus named in such prayers was humbler than that, willing to lose himself without remainder in the least of these, remain unnamed even before Pilate, present especially among those who lack the power to speak for themselves.

Respectfully, get the name of Jesus out of your mouths in such meetings. Focus on truth and honesty. Jesus will be known—if at all—in and through the truth. Because authoritarianism the world over thrives on lies upon lies, drawing the name of Jesus close to it tarnishes his good name. Please stop.

FOR FURTHER READING

S. Claiborne, *Common Prayer: A Liturgy For Ordinary Radicals*, Zondervan, 2012.

7

IS DISCIPLESHIP CRINGY?

Discipleship is a cringy word. Quite a lot of religious language is equally cringy, but you may find the use of discipleship especially egregious because of context. As just one example, the same churches that talk a lot about "discipleship" also feature pages on their web sites introducing their church councils: "businessmen" pictured with their wives.

Right away you learn (from what they show you) that discipleship is primarily a man thing, very heterosexual, directed toward raising a "nuclear" family, middle class and capitalist.

The extent to which discipleship is about authority and control can be seen by considering your position within the discipleship culture. Are you someone "being discipled"? Or are you "discipling"? In almost all formulations of this process, there's a paternalistic dimension verging on the creepy. You can see this illustrated most clearly in local coffee shops in many communities, where older men will be seated across the table from doe-eyed college students, Bibles opened, and the old men explaining to the young women the importance of "submitting to God's will."

Where does one see discussion of "discipleship"? If you are part of a progressive Christian community, you may seldom hear or read the word. But as a progressive pastor who lives adjacent to the dominant evangelical culture, I frequently see it in posts by thought leaders. For these leaders, there is a lot of handwringing over defining the term, questioning whether we do it enough, asking themselves whether, in all their work reaching "the lost" for Christ if they are in fact truly making disciples.

The driving force behind this concern for discipleship is a modern interpretive move prioritizing "the Great Commission" at the conclusion of the gospel of Matthew. The redactor of Matthew's gospel has Jesus saying, during his resurrection appearance, "Go and make disciples of all nations."

This "commission" has been a justifying text for missionary work across the globe. Because it's read as a command (Go!) and because it's Jesus telling the disciples to "make" other disciples, it ends up serving not only as a command but also as an intrinsically patron-client model: "We are disciples, and we are supposed to go make more people like us."

The presumption in this model is that some are already disciples, know what discipleship is, and therefore can pass that on to others. *Must* pass that on to others.

It's hella presumptuous and doesn't take "no" for an answer.

However, in this model, what makes someone "a disciple" remains somewhat unclear, which is why if you google "discipleship" you'll get top hits for "the five marks of disciples," the "four marks of discipleship," the "seven marks of discipleship," the "three Ds of discipleship," etc.

But the assumption is that discipleship is "growing into maturity in Christ." Eventually, if you grow into Christ enough, then presumably you can (and must) then "lead others to Christ." You do this by reading the Bible, submitting to God's will, etc.

Alright, enough of that. I'm sure all the thought-leaders can quibble around the edges of the definition, and will, but what I want to do is try and come at this from a more secular angle of "formation."

I'm going to assume, first, that almost everyone agrees that human beings can mature, grow, learn, develop. Even if you find "discipleship" cringy I bet you are engaged in some form of secular "discipleship" in some aspect of your life. Maybe you are taking piano lessons, or use Duolingo, or are part of a mentorship team at the workplace. In each of these instances, there is a certain body of knowledge, or specific practices, that you believe you can get better at, or learn, through an intentional relationship and/or rehearsal.

However, there are a couple of ways that Christian "discipleship" is set apart from these secular formation practices. First, it's inviting emulation of one particular person (Jesus), which is kind of unusual: I mean I guess there are Elvis Presley impersonators, and some people probably want to be just like RBG, but mostly when we talk about formation in other contexts its formation into a kind of role or profession, or for a skill or knowledge set.

Second, it's assumed this specific formation is a requirement for everyone. Everyone is supposed to be a disciple. I guess like everybody is supposed to brush their teeth.

So why then is discipleship so creepy? I think it boils down to the way in which when the term is popularly used it means formation into a narrow "form of life," whereas if we are to examine discipleship and its goal truly in the way of Jesus, **discipleship is precisely *not* guidance into a narrow form of life but rather anti-guidance into radical freedom.**

I'll need to unpack that.

We can start by quoting Bonhoeffer's popular book on *Discipleship*, which is a book-length examination of the Sermon on the Mount. At one point he writes,

Discipleship is not limited to what you can comprehend—it must transcend all comprehension. Plunge into the deep waters beyond your own comprehension, and I will help you to comprehend even as I do. Bewilderment is the true comprehension. Not to know where you are going is the true knowledge.

If you consider the Beatitudes (included in the Sermon on the Mount) you can understand why Bonhoeffer emphasizes bewilderment. The Beatitudes make statements that are beyond comprehension. Like, "Blessed are the poor." "Blessed are those who mourn." "Blessed are the persecuted."

This is the opening sermon of Jesus, remember, the same guy who will, just a few short chapters later, be arrested and crucified on a cross. A guy who never marries, never opens a successful business, who never figures out how to secure a mortgage and buy a house. And whose own male disciples at the time of his death scattered, betrayed him, and largely misunderstood the teachings they'd been receiving in word and deed over the course of a couple of years.

All of this is to say, if a community is going to attempt to be imitators of Christ, literally, then such a community will not look like most of the communities in our culture that throw the word "discipleship" around with alacrity.

So a thesis: *Discipleship will almost always be found under the form of its opposite.*

I think this is why quite frequently we see examples of "true" discipleship in surprising places, at surprising moments, performed by surprising people, and why a hallmark of actual discipling communities may be their reluctance to even use that term. Because honestly even though that Great Commission text is read as a "must," the real nature of discipleship means whatever it is that it produces cannot be churned out like a Model T on the assembly line.

It's too *free* for that. Both in the economic and existential sense of that term.

Instead, we might say that we are invited into a consideration of how "living like Jesus" will always catch us by surprise because Jesus himself was a surprising figure to his community (both the empire and the religious establishment *and* his own disciples).

We will have to consider that, as much as in a community like a progressive church we will want to form our youth, and be formed together, into certain practices of resistance, certain commitments and ways of living in the world, nevertheless humans will be humans and inasmuch as our particular human community strives to live like the "truly Human One" (Jesus), we will catch the world, ourselves, and one another by surprise.

What does this mean in practice? I think what it might primarily mean is that a) we can consider some of our formation practices as themselves "discipleship" just with less of the cringy religiosity of the traditional use of that term (I'm thinking here of anti-racism work, or environmental activism, or the lifelong struggle to disentangle ourselves from the tempting hegemony of neoliberalism), and b) the primary form "discipleship" actually will take is a critique of all the other discipleships. By which I mean discipleship in Jesus is simply listening to Jesus when he says, "You're more free than you think."

FOR FURTHER READING

E. Enns and C. Myers, *Healing Haunted Histories: A Settler Dicscipleship of Decolonization*, Cascade Books, 2021

8

QUOTE UNQUOTE "PASTOR"

Every sign, linguistic or nonlinguistic, spoken or written (in the usual sense of this opposition), as a small or large unity, can be cited, put between quotation marks; thereby it can break with every given context, and engender infinitely new contexts in an absolutely nonsaturable fashion. This does not suppose that the mark is valid outside its context, but on the contrary that there are only contexts without any center of absolute anchoring.

—Jacques Derrida, on "quotation marks"

C lergy occupy an unusual position in the progressive church. In some progressive groups (like Friends/Quakers), there aren't any clergy. I'm assuming some other peace churches committed to non-hierarchical forms of governance probably lack them also in the traditional sense.

But among most progressive churches, located as they are within the landscape of "mainline Protestants," clergy are indeed a driving force in Christian progressivism. For better or worse, like much of the rest of the Christian world, there is a dynamic interplay between clergy and congregation, with a heavy burden on the clergy to maintain and lead the vitality of the congregation.

But ... as regards the breaking of context for the word "pastor"—which signifies that many Christians who aren't progressive doubt whether progressive pastors "count" as pastors—I often receive the "pastor" title in the way described above, "engendering infinitely new contexts in an absolutely nonsaturable fashion."

Which is why I put the title of this post in quotations. This is a nod to all the critics (there are many) who when they speak of progressive pastors consistently put "pastor" in scare quotes. I salute you!

I concede the point that how we move in the world may not line up with the expected or typical movement of a pastor. I move sideways, if you will, sometimes showing up in surprising spaces.

It's like when a kid runs into their teacher at the grocery store and says, "What are you doing "here"?!" I guess as I've wandered deeper and deeper into this thing called pastoring, I've simply felt called to tuck into some lesser explored rooms and turn the lights on.

I don't spend all my time in these side rooms, mind you. Accompany me for a day, and part of the time you're going to find me preaching and chanting Sunday mornings, spending time visiting the sick, counseling those who seek care, playing with kids at youth group, taking communion to the home-bound, all the things you imagine pastors have done since forever.

Where things go sideways, the times I'm most likely to earn those quotation marks around "pastor", are myriad. They begin with simple cultural, political, and social commitments. Radical affirmation of LGBTQIA people, forwarding socialist political principles, preaching universal salvation, valuing multi-faith participation, favoring prison abolition, etc.

Much of pastoring is inevitably related to the personality of the "person" who is the pastor. I believe that must be an accepted part of pastoring. You need to be yourself. If according to the Strengthsfinder inventory my personality type is high on ideation and connection, then it's no surprise some of our way of being progressive church includes starting new organizations and connecting them deeply to the local community.

However, because I'm radically on the left, and committed to living that radical leftist vision in public as public church and public pastoring, and because doing those things are somewhat unusual for pastors, I think some who see this kind of practice wonder if that's the *main* thing I do, and then wonder if I'd be better off working as a community organizer or non-profit E.D.

But (and this is totally a vocational aside, a sort of model answer to the question, "But what are you called to do?"), I've never felt called to become the E.D. of a non-profit or sign up for community organizing. Or run for office. I'm a pastor.

In traditional, biblical terms I'm doing the bridge-building work that is sometimes referred to "apostolic." My tent-making work is pastoring. These are terms frequently implemented in some church contexts, and I chafe at them because they are often highly gendered: apostles, prophets, evangelists, shepherds, and teachers are the classic list. But I do think it's somewhat accurate to say I pastor in the apostolic mode.

As I have increasingly attended to the writings of liberation theologians and analysts of the subaltern (those of "lower status"); as I've taken into account the class analyses of socialists; and as I ponder the breadth of classes I've inhabited (rural farming, academia, small town pastoring, urban life), more and more I've felt it was important for clergy to get embedded in the daily life of working people.

This is one reason I asked our church council in 2021 if I could start substitute teaching. I wanted to help alleviate a crisis in the culture, a shortage of teachers and subs. I also wanted to get closer to school life and spend time with young people. The traditional churchy way to do that would be to try and do more youth programs at the church. But we aren't hyperfocused on programs at our church, and everyone's already too busy as it is. Subbing gets me into the nitty gritty.

It also opens some unique opportunities. Because I'm subbing AND have a community voice as a pastor, I can use that voice to advocate for better wages for subs and other classified school staff.

The same holds true for some of the non-profits we have started. As a result of starting Queer Camp at our church, I'm honored to be in touch with youth queer culture and can advocate for their needs *in solidarity with them* in ways I couldn't if I had simply preached about inclusion without practicing it.

The one problem this presents for congregational life (and it's a rather big problem) is the congregation can sometimes wonder, "How is this new emerging thing for us?" It can come as a bit of a shock when, at least for a period as a new thing is launched, the worship and announcements and energy of some of the volunteers and the energy of the pastor are all focused on the launch of the new.

This was certainly true when we started Canopy NWA, a non-profit that has now grown into the main refugee resettlement center for the state of Arkansas. Until we got the funding together to hire our first E.D., there was a six-month period when I was half-time organizing the refugee resettlement org and half-time pastoring.

But, and this is crucial, a lot of this has to do with perceptions of time, and how ministry (and any kind of social justice work) occurs *over time*. If you can wait long enough, you as the parishioner will likely see the benefit to you as a member. In the case of refugee resettlement, what emerged over the long haul were opportunities to volunteer with co-sponsor teams for arriving refugees, and now, a few years into it, many new neighbors to know and love from across the planet.

Similarly with the launch of Ozark Atolls, our Marshallese ministry, back during the beginning of the pandemic. Sometimes you just jump into something because it's the right thing to do, and when we knew we could help and we knew

Marshallese were dying and struggling with COVID, we knew what to do.

Now, two years in, we've begun to realize what started as an emergency response to crisis is becoming our main practice of Christian reparations. We offer our space, our time, our resources, to a community of people who suffered tremendous harm from our testing of nuclear weapons on their islands. As a congregation, we can't repair all that harm, but entering into this partnership repairs a little bit.

Such pastoring in action can be perceived as "divisive." Advocating for the subaltern will always be perceived as divisive. Speaking up for and standing in solidarity with oppressed communities is inherently divisive, because the power of the status quo will see it as such.

Take as an example Arkansas passing anti-trans legislation denying health care access to trans youth. A middle non-divisive response to this would be to try and work in the middle, bringing to the table the needs of trans youth AND the concerns of legislators.

Except, in this case, the concerns of legislators are completely at odds with the recommendations of the medical community and originate in hate and transphobia. As a pastor, I believe there is no other way to act in the face of hate than to stand in solidarity with those suffering from the hate and suffer with them. In fact, I think it's a part of pastoral ministry (this is good shepherding) to draw some of the heat away and toward yourself.

It's one thing for trans youth and their parents to stand up for themselves. It's a whole other thing when a wider community not directly impacted by the legislation stands up for them also. And it's a whole other thing again to turn the attack back around and into a fight and name the legislators as immoral and bigoted. Which they are.

To say these kinds of things, to say them out loud, to keep repeating them, to not back down. To believe that is good pastoring. This is part of what earns the quotation marks.

I'll conclude with one simple observation: all pastors who use social media are now navigating ministry in a way different from their predecessors. It's why I like to talk about this work as open-source and public. Social media has made it possible for a parish to get a glimpse into the life of pastors in a way unprecedented compared to previous generations. For better or worse, my congregation and a lot of my wider community knows not only my political views but also about the games I like to play and the food I eat.

I've certainly made some mistakes along the way, maybe over-sharing or stating more briefly and starkly what should have been a long-form essay. When you get angry and Twitter is just a few taps away, that's part of the new ministry landscape.

But this too is part of pastoring. It's why I first joined social media when I got that personal invite from Mark Zuckerberg (*wink*) and have never looked back. Shepherds spend time where the sheep are.

I'm still uncertain some days about whether shepherd is a good metaphor for the role of pastor in a community, but it is how a congregation tends to think of its pastor (I know mine does, despite my continuing tendencies toward chaos pastoring). I guess we live with it as an archetype while also listening to the God who in Christ did not think of being like God as something to be grasped, but instead took on the form of a servant. Until somebody finally figures out the Holy Grail of a self-actuating group, I think we'll always see the Spirit at work in the interplay between "leader" and people, hopefully never with too much focus on the leader, but just enough to make it about "the people."

I want to be that kind of "pastor."

FOR FURTHER READING

T. Gorringe, *Alan Ecclestone, Priest As Revolutionary*, Cairns Publications, 1994.

FREIDIGKEIT: BRAZEN FREEDOM

I f you survey a cross-section of Lutherans and ask them to name the special focus of Lutheran theology, the most common response you'll receive is, "Grace."

If you ask me to give you one word that indicates what is central to Lutheran theology, I'd offer an alternative: "Freedom."

Admittedly, both words will do, and both do indicate aspects of Lutheran theology that, although not exclusively Lutheran, are certainly key terms for Lutherans as compared to other traditions.

However, the reason to prioritize freedom over grace, and do so every time, is because grace is pious and church-y whereas freedom is earthy and more secular.

There's an old German word—*Freidigkeit*. Dorothee Solle says she learned the word from Friedrich Gogarten, one of her theology professors. It's the term Martin Luther used to translate the Greek New Testament term *parrhesia*. *Freidigkeit* "is often rendered as free-oppenness, free-mindedness, venturesome confidence; Gogarten told us that it was a melding of 'freedom' (*Freiheit)* and '"brazenness' (*Frechheit*) ... but heaven help the student who interpreted this magnificent term with the clerical sentiment of 'joyfulness.' This would infuriate Gogarten, who utterly detested any kind of churchy drivel" (*Against the Wind*, 23).

What some find so troubling about "progressive" Christianity is its "bold freedom," its *Freidigkeit*. There is a kind of freedom in no longer worrying overly much about salvation. It can be emboldening to slough off all threats that this or that action might "damn you to hell for all eternity."

There's even a colloquial adjective for this in English: "Devil-may-care." This is particularly on-point for all those whose freedom has been constrained by the threat, regularly articulated in their communities, of "going to hell."

Returning to the Greek term *parrhesia* Luther was translating, it can also be translated as "bold speech," "free speech," speech unbounded by normal rules either of polite conduct or context. In fact, true *parrhesia* is bound the other direction, bound not by the dictates of custom or concern, but rather bound to speak the truth for the common good, even at personal risk.

Whatever word you want to use for this kind of freedom, it's sorely needed in a world threatened by authoritarianism and fascism, in religious communities where freedom of speech and action has been so dramatically curtailed through multiple systems: bourgeoise custom, capitalist demands, and systems of religious control.

Many Christians feel hemmed in on all sides, controlled by many forces. In fact many Christians don't even realize how much they are controlled. They sit around asking themselves whether doing or saying this or that will gather too much attention to them, or change a friendship, or untether a belief they've been clinging to. All these questions, spoken or not, batter away at our souls.

But the reality of God's Spirit leads us out of these kinds of false questions. It leads us into bold forms of truth, in action and speech. The old Lutheran phrase has always been, *Sin boldly*. The progressive Christian approach is probably more like "don't let the religious bastards drag you down"—by which we might mean parts of Scripture that are misogynistic, parts of Christian tradition that maintained bigotry, modern forms of religiosity that were/are intrinsically racist, etc.

Instead, be free. Speak boldly. Be venturesome and confident "come hell or high water."

Progressive church constantly risks this. It breaks church and social norms with some regularity, including an articulated openness to practices and traditions outside of Christianity. Progressive Christians are willing to be identified with and speak out for those anathematized by "traditional" Christians, whether that's queer people or Socialists or those in prison or those currently unhoused.

This kind of free speech sometimes (admittedly) pushes the

envelope. A few years back some colleagues of mine actually published an Advent devotional titled "Fuck This Shit." It's still up online, you might even use it this year.

Keep in mind, Trump had just been elected. It was the prayer everyone was praying in progressive church circles even if they didn't always say it out loud.

Swearing is important for a variety of reasons, not least of which because it is authentic speech, but also because it transgresses traditional class boundaries. There's a certain kind of respectability enforced in middle-class culture, and part of that respectability is related to how we talk. Since the church is mostly in captivity to middle class sensibilities, one fast way to indicate I'm not "that kind of pastor" is simply to swear. It shocks the system in a way quite different than if you were at a construction site.

Progressives are in favor of free speech and think the church should indeed do away with the faux piety that worries about swearing more than it worries about people being homeless or starving.

This kind of bold freedom is, as the original Greek term signified, best exercised bound to the common good even at personal risk.

In Luther's classic *The Freedom of a Christian*, he laid out a paradox:

A Christian is utterly free, lord of all, subject to none.

A Christian is utterly dutiful, servant of all, subject to all.

What Luther meant here is complex (it's a paradox, after all, and also, he wrote a whole book about it), but essentially because of who God is in relationship to us we are now free (in Christ) and then precisely in that freedom "in Christ" we become servants of all (like Christ).

Progressive Christianity can sometimes veer in a puritanical direction. However, a lot of the time these moves toward what is perceived as puritanical are more exercises in *Freidigkeit/Parrhesia*. That is, they are bold exercises in freedom that are bound in neighbor love.

A specific example: Our church hosts a Queer Camp for queer youth because the wider Christian culture around us has regularly been passing bigoted laws that harm queer youth (trans youth in particular). The bold freedom we exercise as a Christian community to speak out against such bigotry and to host radically caring spaces like Queer Camp arises out of this paradox.

We are free to love queer youth just as they are without trying to convert or change them (this probably surprises most traditional Christians); we are bound to love queer youth just as they are because we want to live like Christ and as free as Christ is.

The exercise of such bold freedom is an ongoing journey, especially for those previously traumatized in religious community that practiced multiple forms of social control. Almost all of us have been shaped by some kinds of social control (bourgeoise normativity, the strictures of capitalism, cisnormativity, etc.) so in a way *Freidigkeit* is an ongoing way for all of us. But those processing their religious trauma will find this whole topic both very freeing and also ... hard.

Let's include here at the end a bit of meditation on that last part of the definition of *parrhesia*, the "even at personal risk" part.

It's not easy to organize a religious community that is willing to take personal risks. Most progressives would like to be somewhat proximate to organizations that take such risks, but most of us will then also distance ourselves if things get too difficult.

Social justice organizers the world over know the powerful use their power to shatter organizing movements. They're quite skillful at it and know exactly the pressure points to push.

It's hard to get those working in corporate offices to protest in solidarity with line workers if their income is at risk. It's hard to speak the truth at home if your family will then shun you. Even pastors who regularly engage in relatively *more* progressive action than moderate churches nevertheless do the mental calculations on whether this or that action, this or that form of speech, will result in us not being able to keep a roof over our family's heads.

It's also difficult to speak the truth for the common good if the voices inside your own head sing a chorus of self-doubt.

In the end, this is reason to value the sometimes-overlooked part of Luther's paradoxical articulation of the freedom of a Christian. It's specifically the freedom "of a Christian." That is to say, we keep in mind that we are free "in Christ." This becomes both source and norm of our bold freedom.

This is true both at the sociological and the eschatological level. At the sociological level our bold freedom resides in joining (and reminding ourselves that we are part of) the body of Christ, so that what may feel like personal risk is simply solidarity with communities who are forced to live that risk all the time even if we are free to enter into the same risks only when we so choose.

The eschatological part is related to ultimate risk: that because we are in Christ there is no "ultimate" risk of taking personal risks for our neighbors. By ultimate risk here I do mean mortal risk: because we are saved for life with God we are already free now to not worry over this life in quite the same way others do. This last part is especially freeing and was why Christians like Martin Luther King Jr. or Dorothee Sølle were not, in the end, worried about the personal risk, because they were in Christ, unafraid to die, and therefore already truly free.

And there's nothing at all more boldly free than that.

FOR FURTHER READING

D. Soelle, *Against the Wind: Memoirs of a Radical Christian*, Fortress Press, 1999.

10

IF JESUS WAS JUST A REALLY GREAT GUY, WHY DO WE WORSHIP HIM?

L et's lean into the whole topic of the creed and Christ's divinity a little bit more because it's crucial for an understanding of any kind of progressive movement we also name "Christian." However, it's somewhat treacherous working this space because there are honestly a lot of conflicted thoughts (and feelings) about it in progressive circles.

Perhaps the most popular writer today tilling the progressive fields and Christology is Richard Rohr. Many of you reading this chapter may also subscribe to his Daily Meditations from the Center for Action and Contemplation, so it will come as a sort-of surprise if I then go on immediately to state unequivocally that I have major reservations with his project, especially with his recent *The Universal Christ*.

The whole discussion of Jesus as God and as human has kept Christian theology busy ever since, well, since ever. It's *the* topic in Christology, and Christian thought more generally. So this post can't be an entire survey of the whole history of the development and continuing maintenance of the *homoousion* (the theological concept of Jesus being the same in being, same in essence as God the Father).

The overly simplistic way to describe this term is to remember that every kind of Christianity and every heresy has at root been a back and forth along a continuum between "Jesus was just a man who God really liked" all the way over to "God in Christ wasn't really a man he just played one on TV ... he was really just God." Along that continuum have been thousands of proposals, some better and some worse, finding words to spell out the mystery of Jesus Christ being both fully God and fully human.

In brief: I fundamentally disagree with Richard Rohr's claim that the spirit of Christ is not the same as the person of Jesus, because he erroneously lets go of the paradoxical tension of those two "fully"s.

Quite the opposite of Rohr, I think a stronger progressive Christian perspective is to maintain that Jesus really is truly the Christ, the eternal Logos, God from God and light from light, of one being with the Father, etc. happily repeating from memory all the parts of the Nicene Creed and believing them.

Now, this does not mean progressives need to reject all of Richard Rohr's work. Not at all. In Rohr we have a spiritual leader arising out of progressive Roman Catholicism who offers excellent resources for action and reflection.

But like many theologians before him, he's traveling the

wrong road to get to the destination he intends. It's problematic to divide Jesus from "the Christ" in this manner precisely because the most radical parts of Scripture point to this Christ as being fully present in this one specific person, Jesus. Yes, it's part of the offense of the gospel that God is fully invested and present in this one specific Palestinian Jew. And ... that's precisely how Christ is "cosmic."

The early church was at such great lengths to work out a clear articulation of how Jesus was "of one being with the Father" because the authority of everything Jesus said and did is related to who he was. And it's not just later church tradition that worried itself over this. The discussion has been around ever since the Centurion at Christ's crucifixion is reported to have said (in Matthew): "Truly this is God's Son." Then that dialogue kept going three days later when the women left the tomb and told the disciples, "He's not there."

All of this is narrative/gospel of how we are to think of Jesus Christ as "Son of God." What Jesus taught (from his parables to his sermons) and did (from his healing to his prophetic actions) all gain their gravity out of who he is in Scripture: the one in whom God dwelt fully.

The *homoousious* (of one being with) makes the Sermon on the Mount vital. We find Christ's preaching and life so profoundly compelling precisely because it was God in Jesus doing all those things and saying all those things.

All progressive Christianity that is not liberal Christianity in disguise (we'll need to discuss "liberal" Christianity in a separate chapter) is distinguished by its maintaining a commitment to this truth, that the Christ isn't "divine" just because he is perceived by us as good but instead the opposite, we learn "the good" that is Christ's preferential option for the poor in and through coming to faith that the Christ who modeled this preferential option was/is "Son of God."

It's important to keep in mind this claim, that Jesus was of one being with the Father, is not made as an authoritarian move to squash all opposition. If we attend to the historical context for when this was all being worked out, we can keep in mind that such an assertion places any community who believes it at risk in precisely the same way Jesus' life was at risk. To believe that Jesus was "LORD" was to set up a "LORD" in opposition to other "LORDs."

In the 21st century, given what we now know about this kind of language and the function and place of "LORDs", we may rightly struggle with the term—but it is profoundly helpful to remember that Jesus is only named "Lord" as a way of indicating Jesus was in opposition to all the other "Lords," from the religious leaders to Caesar himself.

In the present moment, with the rise of authoritarianism and Christian nationalism, how much more important to keep this in mind, because the peculiar way Jesus was a "Lord" was in solidarity with all the communities of peoples that authoritarianism and Christian nationalism now wish to erase or reduce or sideline.

The problem with Christian progressives abandoning a faith commitment to the "of one being with" is then they no longer have any theological perspective that provides support for their actions and teachings. They have no connection to any kind of "sovereignty" in the positive sense of that word. As a friend recently wrote, "Divine sovereignty is a doctrine of comfort: If the God revealed in Jesus is sovereign, then Caesar is not, which sounds like very good news to me."

Just so we might say the greatest resistance to authoritarianism is the maintenance of the homoousion. Authoritarians think the authority they can enforce is "of one being with the Father." Thank God we know that "of one being with" is in Jesus.

FOR FURTHER READING
E. Käsemann, *Jesus Means Freedom*, Fortress Press, 1969.

PART III

BELIEF

11

IS FORGIVENESS POSSIBLE? ~OR~ IS IT STRUGGLE ALL THE WAY DOWN?

A re there some wrongs that can never be righted? Which is to say, is forgiveness possible?

Many of us recognize that past harms have repercussions over generations, especially when very little has been done to truly redress them. Think of European settlement and genocide in the Americas. Many institutions are now making "land acknowledgments" as a way of raising awareness and expressing complicity. Some churches and denominations are repudiating the Doctrine of Discovery (a religious, political and legal justification for colonization and seizure of land that was not inhabited by Christians). But those making such statements are also aware these are small steps, tentative and inadequate, if the goal is truly seeking forgiveness and practicing reparations.

Much the same could be said for the contemporary conversation about slavery and the call for African American reparations. Before much repair has even been offered, we are already tempted to ask ourselves: how much is enough?

Part of the reason the struggle for social justice is a perpetual struggle has to do, it seems, with the reality that those causing the harm only very rarely fully confess what they've done, and then also resist repairing the damage. This is why, for example, mega-corporations are often willing to accept multi-million-dollar fines after long and costly court battles—they know the fines will still be dwarfed by the profits.

In other words, the perpetual struggle is still profitable for those in power, and as a result they see little reason to "do the work" because the costs outweigh the benefits. The work is easy, and the conscience is untroubled because the pockets are lined and lives comfortable.

The struggle is also perpetual for those seeking justice because their pain is so great, the grief and tragedy unremitting, the memory of the lost or harmed resonant, and because the cause is just. This is righteous action, re-establishing right relationships between neighbors and creation. Who can give up on that?

However, let's pause here briefly and note that this is repair/struggle, forgiveness all within the immanent frame—the this-worldly, human frame. Thus far the question is whether things can ever be made right between humans and the rest of creation, and if so, how much would need to be done to accomplish it?

We should add that in Christian perspective, there is an additional frame, one that plays less a part of the imagination of progressive Christians than some other groups. In addition to whether forgiveness can be accomplished between humans or groups, whether reparations can ever be fully realized, we might also ask ourselves whether or not forgiveness and repair can ever truly happen *before God*.

Answering this question well becomes a resource both for hope and expanded repair. If we are stuck in cycles of injustice, it may behoove us to ask ourselves whether or not forgiveness accomplished "in Christ" and "before God" may themselves radically shift how we think about forgiveness in the immanent frame itself.

In Lutheran theology we say, based on the immensely influential *Small Catechism*, that confession is "for the sake of the absolution." Everything hinges for Luther on the forgiveness side of the equation. Even in another article in the catechism, on the Eucharist, Luther can say that those who are worthy to receive the sacrament are those who simply trust that it is "for them for the forgiveness of sins."

As regards confession, Luther wants to ensure that the sinner does not overly agonize over attempting to enumerate all their sins (something that was sometimes demanded in the Roman Catholic confessional culture of the time), but rather simply to list the sins that burdened them, and then trust the words of absolution "as if from God themself." The word of absolution is a freeing word, one with power, precisely *because* it frees.

Okay, let's return to forgiveness and reparations in the immanent frame. First, we must acknowledge that it is not the role of the one who has caused the harm to define the terms of forgiveness. That is up to the one (or community) wronged. So, in what follows I am not giving out any assignments. I'm only thinking through how to process my own responsibilities to forgive and repair.

On a practical level, we can say that forgiveness happens if the one wronged expresses forgiveness, or accepts the offered repair. This becomes more difficult to define when the wrongs have been committed against those who are already dead, or against creation itself, or are systemic in nature. In all of those situations the question remains: how much is enough?

In relationship to this question, we are weak, inadequate to the task. We cannot repair it all, find all the people from whom we could seek forgiveness, or in the case of creation extract a verbal expression of forgiveness. We share instead with God in Christ as part of creation a kind of weakness in this regard.

Consider what my friend Greg Walter says about this. In his *Being Promised*, he writes, "weak power gives possibility directed toward the neighbor. It is open to public criticism and evaluation. Promise occupies no place and gives the place to the neighbor, requiring a radical kind of hospitality" (13).

In an interview he conducted around the time his book came out, he had this to say:

> All eschatology is local.
>
> Since God's promise is always other-directed, since the place of promise is always the place of the other, any statements we make about eschatology or fulfillment are always bound to the neighbor.
>
> In other words, I think that a kind of cosmic or total eschatology is a bit over-hasty. We might be able to articulate that from God's promise but I think what we have biblically-speaking is the apocalyptic seer's poetry, parabolic statements in the Gospels, and various wisdom sayings throughout Paul. When taken from the perspective of promise, we have just a schema, a bare-bones skeleton that has flesh only when it is addressed to the neighbor's needs, concerns, and injuries.
>
> Eschatological claims need to be filled out in relationship to the way that God's promise in Jesus addresses those local concerns. Thus, it is not just enough to be a theologian of the cross, you need to be a local theologian of the cross. And that isn't enough either because the theology of the cross needs this promise in order to get the openness and spirit-breathed impossibility interwoven into the local scene.

This may be an overly simplistic interpretation, but in a sense what he is saying is: Do what you can, then trust (or hope?). And stay local.

The future that happens *after* we seek forgiveness or offer reparations is not up to us, or controlled by us. It is not a specific place we are heading, as if there is already a place and God's Spirit is inviting us there. Rather, "the Spirit is the future itself, a welcome that allows one to expect the unexpected" (54).

Forgiveness and repair in the immanent frame are super-saturated, filled with the possibility of the "more" of God's forgiveness while all under the aegis of the weak power of what can be done.

Which is to say: *Go ahead and start.* You're right, your church is never going to be able to create a fund for every kind of reparations that is needed. Your worry that what you do or what is demanded will never be enough should be no barrier to beginning or continuing. If you have a conversation about repa-rations for African American churches, inevitably someone will ask if you should also fund reparations for Native Americans. And probably we should. But what-aboutism is a logical fallacy, not a constructive theology of holistic forgiveness.

The steps on the way to forgiveness and repair are not a zero-sum game, a narrow path where each fork in the road is a direction lost once one is chosen. Rather, the steps on the way are creative, and much like a garden, may bear the most fruit if applied in specific soil right in the back yard.

And some of the practices that may lead to forgiveness, some of the practices that are repair, may first have to take the form of promises. This is why ultimately documents like the repudiation of the doctrine of discovery are not received as purely empty words, but words with potential. They are a kind of promise.

Walter again: "A true promise is weak. It is an adventure. Making a promise is risky but so is trusting one. This means a kind of waiting on what may come, that which comes-to, advent. This life is a risk, an opening, and a willingness to see what happens" (personal correspondence).

The bravery to accept this risk is a kind of courage to embrace the fragility of oneself and each other. Mary Oliver has a line: "I tell you this to *break* your *heart*, by which I mean only that it *break* open and never close again to the rest of the world." I think that is the risk of promise, which is to dwell in this life of Spirit that the Crucified One pledges.

Is forgiveness possible? If we are going to answer responsibly, we can answer weakly: maybe.

Is it struggle all the way down? I hope not.

Is extending a promise that may be broken, that illustrates our fragility, that really ventures something, worth it?

I mean, that's who Jesus was, right? He is that kind of promise from God.

That's the theological turn in terms of "making right" that I believe can provide resources for those of us seeking to make things right in the immanent frame.

In other words, I do not honestly know whether the steps I take, the promises I make, to work to repair the harm that has occurred through the various systems in which I am complicit will ever be enough. But getting to that level, to gaining such purview, is not my responsibility, even if some kinds of progressivism aim that high.

Progressive church begins where it can, and meets the gift of God, Jesus, in its willingness to risk and see what happens.

FOR FURTHER READING
G. Walter, *Being Promised: Theology, Gift, and Practice*, Eerdmans, 2013

12

A DETOUR INTO DEMYTHOLOGIZATION (ESPECIALLY NEOLIBERALISM)

This guidebook has been noticeably relying on certain theological guides. Chief among them have been Dietrich Bonhoeffer, Martin Luther King Jr., and Dorothee Soelle, but another theologian and New Testament scholar who really cracked open so much for me as a progressive thinker and practitioner has been Ernst Käsemann (yes, they're all of the 20th century). Specifically, his reflections on what it means to follow Christ, or in his terms, to "be a disciple of the crucified Nazarene."

What precisely does it mean to be a disciple of the crucified Nazarene? He offers this definition: "True surrender of the disciple is unbound, not a private affair, tends toward aid to the world, extends freedom everywhere" (128).

This is the outward manifestation, but this definition of discipleship can only be understood in the context of discipleship as spiritual warfare, an essentially apocalyptic approach to understanding biblical interpretation and the Christian life.

Käsemann suggests in his writings that we should, in Huguenot style call out: 'Résistez!'

He writes:

> Discipleship of the Crucified leads necessarily to resistance to idolatry on every front. This resistance is and must be the most important mark of Christian freedom" (xxi). So, discipleship is always resistance to idolatry, and this is precisely because the spiritual life always has something as its lord, is always ridden, either by Jesus or the lords of this world. "There is no neutral zone between gospel and idol worship. Whoever is not for the one lives for the other" (87). "What is assumed is an anthropology that defines one at any given time by one's lord (131).

Readers unfamiliar with Käsemann but somewhat familiar with the project of demythologization will know it is about making the move (in biblical interpretation) out of previous mythologies that no longer sustain and connect instead to a more modern view of the world. But for Käsemann this is not precisely about bursting the bubble of antiquated mythologies; rather demythologization is not simply something that is done in relation to the Bible, but to all contexts needing to be demythologized—especially, he makes a point of noting, one way of reading Scripture that needs to be demythologized is the Enlightenment readings of Scripture themselves.

In fact, almost all readers of Scripture and preachers would benefit from memorizing his definition of demythologization: "In the evangelical sense demythologizing occurs as a battle and resistance against superstition. And superstition, at least according to Luther's explanation of the first commandment, is 'everything that does not allow us most deeply and without compromise to fear, love and trust God above all things.' Thus demythologizing, evangelically conceived and rooted [evangelical here in the older sense of "good news" rather than American evangelical], denotes ridding humanity and the earth of the demonic" (200). Demythologization does not claim that demons don't exist—rather, it does battle with the demons.

One such "demon" in the world today is our anxiety. So in some of his later essays he considers the relationship between apocalyptic and anxiety, and proceeds to do so by demythologizing both. In the end, he shows how true Christian apocalyptic does not cause anxiety, but is the antidote for it, whereas worldly anxiety misinterprets the apocalyptic and fails to see how it is the carrier of evangelical freedom and truth.

We can find parallels to this understanding of apocalyptic in the work even of secular thinkers and performers. Most recently I watched a performance by Bread and Puppets, the oldest and longest-performing political puppet theater in the nation, founded in 1963 in Vermont. They put on a performance in our church, and the title was "Apocalypse Defiance Circus." They made use of the tropes and political tendencies of apocalyptic itself to fight back against the aspect of the apocalyptic that in another sense raises our anxiety.

A major focus of Käsemann throughout his essays is a call

to the "white race" to acknowledge its complicity in the sufferings of the world (remarkable given his status as a mid-20th century German theologian). This leitmotif can be found in almost every essay he wrote. He pushes the topic of race to such a degree because he firmly believes that the church of Jesus Christ should be "a resistance movement of the exalted Lord against all who make God's creation a prison for anyone, near or far, a playground for their selfishness, vanity, and lust for rule" (277).

This framing is helpful. It's mythological in its demythologization which may make us squirm a bit, but it's convincing in operating under the assumption that there are massive forces in our world (forces like racism, neoliberalism, patriarchy, ecological degradation) that indeed make God's creation a prison. It implements some of what sound like the same religious tropes critics of progressive church implement but toward the empowerment of those previously imprisoned.

"We live in a utopia: it just isn't ours," writes China Miéville, one of the great imaginative critics of contemporary capitalism.

A (largely) pejorative term I find useful even if difficult to define that gathers up all the problems of capitalism encapsulated in Miéville's pithy, ironic comment is *neoliberalism*. Let's keep the definition simple to start: neoliberalism is the transformation of society as a result of market-based reforms, and in its pejorative mode it is the transformations that put tremendous pressure on everyone in every way with no escape available. In the context of pastoral ministry, I have special concerns about the dismissal of care and care cultures in the context of neoliberalism.

Neoliberal economics is working wonderfully for the wealthiest 1 percent. As Oxfam reports, 82 percent of all the world's wealth went to the richest 1 percent in 2017. The world's wealth simply isn't for most people.

Theologian and psychotherapist Bruce Rogers-Vaughn agrees. He wonders (based on a keyword search in the ATLA religion database) why theological studies have remained essentially silent on the topic of neoliberalism, while the social sciences have seen a sevenfold increase in mention of the topic between 1990 and 2014. He finds this failure unfortunate, not only because it avoids addressing a root cause of suffering but also because such silence is likely a form of collusion. Accordingly, his book offers a class-centered critique of contemporary capitalism and its devastating effect on the souls he encounters as a pastoral counselor and psychotherapist.

Neoliberalism, Rogers-Vaughn believes, is the hegemonic and all-encompassing factor in shaping why and how humans suffer. He defines it as a development in capitalism, most of whose advocates emphasize freedom, which is generally characterized by the "unimpeded functioning of markets." It has created a "global hegemony that does not look like a hegemony, one that claims to be a liberator of humankind even as it shackles the human soul" (42).

Rogers-Vaughn observes a marked change in the people he

sees now in his practice compared to 30 years ago. His patients are more on edge, experiencing an amorphous dread. The selves he encounters are more diffuse and fragmented, prone to greater levels of addictive behavior, haunted by shame and loneliness, unaffiliated, and burdened with many private sufferings. Through long experience and reading in critical literature, he has become convinced that such changes are the result not of individual failures but of large shifts in the form of capitalism practiced in the United States—especially shifts implemented during the 1980s, the era of Thatcher and Reagan.

He writes,

> The challenge of caring for souls is not the effort to fix discrete personal problems or even to redress specific injustices. It is, rather, to aid people, individually and collectively, in finding their footing—to articulate the deep meanings that ground their lives and to strengthen healthy collectives and social movements that hold some residue of transcendent values (128).

Rogers-Vaughn believes that much of therapy and counseling (including pastoral care) colludes with neoliberalism. He identifies collusive care as that which emphasizes *Adaptation* to society (rather than resistance), *functioning* in accord with the values of production and consumption (rather than *communion* and *wholeness* in relation to others and the earth), *symptoms relief* (rather than *meaning-making*), and accepting *personal responsibility* (rather than interdependent reliance within the web of human relationships).

This kind of care addresses relatively well first-order suffering (caused by the human condition, like illness or plague) and second-order suffering (caused by human evil, like war or ecological devastation). But it does not address third-order suffering, "the new chronic," still ill-defined and difficult to name but clearly present as a general malaise in the culture writ large.

Through a rigorous and expansive synthesis of the literature on neoliberalism, Rogers-Vaughn surveys where we are now with hints of where we might go. But his book is by no means a handbook. In fact, he jests, "there is no *Diagnostic and Statistical Manual of Neoliberal Disorders*, coupled with sets of 'best practices' for alleviating the particular distresses they produce." It's likely that he would consider any such handbook a symptom of the disease, not the cure. As he states, "caring for souls requires us to escape these small boxes in which we simply help people manage their suffering."

One small box from which we need to escape is the strategic pitting of class issues and cultural identity against each other. "Part of the success of neoliberalism consists in how effectively it has co-opted the spirit of the 1960s ... It accomplished this by driving a wedge between social justice efforts focused on economic fairness and those emphasizing cultural identities." This co-optation has contributed to the widespread *ressentiment* that fuels modern-day populisms.

Rogers-Vaughn proposes an ecclesiology that envisions the church as communities of the expelled. He believes that neoliberalism is not simply antigovernment and antiunion; it is also antichurch. "One exhibit of this broad dismantling of collectives is the continuing decline of religious institutions in the United States, a steady erosion that signifies the general *marginalization* of religious collectives under neoliberal governance." But he sees the negative energy of neoliberalism against communities of faith as an opportunity to discover once again the core definition of communities centered in the way of Jesus.

What if the church understood itself to be the community of the expelled—all those pushed out by the many forces of neoliberalism, from nationalism to racism to classism and more? This proposal offers a compelling redress to the sense of spiritual homelessness. The expelled are not homeless at all. In the church, they are cast out together, and the care of souls occurs as the community finds life in its collective resistance.

FOR FURTHER READING
E. Käsemann, *On Being a Disciple of the Crucified Nazarene*, Eerdmans, 2010.

13

BEING ECUMENICAL AND INTERFAITH WHILE REMAINING COMMITTED TO TRINITARIAN THEOLOGY

For several years our congregation coordinated a summer Interfaith Camp. Over the course of a week campers visited multiple sites in our city to learn about the Jewish, Christian, Muslim, Buddhist, and Hindu faiths in interfaith perspective.

Because this was a camp for children, we kept to the basics. For many of them, a tour of the synagogue or Islamic Center was their first time visiting such spaces. Perhaps less for Jewish and Muslim participants in the camp who had already visited churches because, well, there's a Christian church on every block in our town. And that's not an exaggeration.

Lots of wonderful, rich and complex work has been done exploring the connection between various faiths. But on a very practical level, people of different faiths lack the most basic experience of simply being in each other's spaces. I'm guessing even many readers of this book may never have visited a synagogue or mosque or attended religious services outside of their own Christian tradition.

For this reason alone, the camp was a real blessing. Not only did campers from many different religious traditions spend a week together making friends: they can also now all say, "Yes, I've been to an Islamic Center. Yes, I've been to a synagogue." And if they were paying attention, they might also know that we have many overlapping traditions (like Abraham is important in Christianity, Judaism, and Islam) and we also do some things differently.

Around the same time our congregation was partnering with area faith communities for Interfaith Camp, we'd also worked to deepen various interfaith practices. For example, during Ramadan the Islamic Center puts on a meal every day at sundown. As a Lutheran congregation we had the chance to prepare one of these meals for them and eat with the community. Similarly, over the years we have coordinated regularly with the synagogue on interfaith prayer vigils, educational events, and visits to one another's worship services.

All these kinds of practices require a certain level of trust and maintenance of caring relationship. In a part of the country where many Christians are attempting to "convert" the Jewish or Muslim communities, it is part of our responsibility as progressive Christians to model a different way, a way of interfaith sharing and, in some instances, multi-faith belonging.

When we practice interfaith community, some may perceive it in overly simplistic fashion. Kind of like, "Well, all religions lead to the same place/goal. It's all good." This is not what I believe or practice.

Interfaith community is about growing in our own faith by being in relationship with other faiths. I don't actually think that a Jew, or a Christian, or a Muslim, or a Buddhist, or a Hindu, all have the same sense of the ultimate, where everything is heading. Each of our eschatologies may differ, and to melt them all together into one homogenous whole is presumptive and problematic.

Instead, what is going on in interfaith dialogue is unity in diversity. A shared kind of curiosity, where a Muslim will not attempt to disabuse a Christian of their Trinitarian sensibilities but rather open a conversation about how the Islamic belief that "there is no God but God" relates to the Jewish *Shema*, the Lord is one, or the Christian creed that God's unity is expressed precisely in Trinity, three in one and one in three.

To be in relationship, you have to *be* somebody. Emptying yourself of all commitments, beliefs, boundaries, simply mimicking the other is no sort of relationship at all at the interpersonal level. So too to practice interfaith relationship, having a sense of what you believe, why you do what you do, who you are, is essential to forming the relationship. And trusting that the one you are relating to also is a "self," an "other." Interfaith relationship is about the coming together of different religious "personalities."

This becomes particularly important when we begin discussing "multiple religious belonging."

It is one of the primary Christian virtues that teaches us to approach other religions hospitably rather than antagonistically. "If Christians are to exercise a virtue that lies at the core of Christian tradition–namely, hospitality–we must be prepared to receive as well as to give" (Thatamanil, 17).

Multiple religious participation has often been characterized by theologians uncharitably as individualistic, simply religious consumers choosing from a smorgasbord of options. But many multiple religious practitioners do so not out of hyperindividualism, but rather out of a deep love for more than one tradition.

I have seen this increasingly in my ministry as a pastor. Not only do I have Christian parishioners who practice yoga. I also have members who attend synagogue, identify as Buddhist, and connect with Islam and other religious traditions. Others understand themselves as pagan and Christian, or even atheist and Christian.

I love the work of John Thatamanil in particular on this point. What I love about his work is its offer of theological equipment for consideration of the ways we learn more about ourselves by learning from others.

He writes, "We can learn to love and love to learn from what is not already our own. After generations of seeking to convert the world and thereby erase religious diversity—a project that has underwritten all manner of colonial violence—the time has come to receive rather than propagate, to reorient Christian communities toward the virtues of humility and hospitality rather than an aggressive 'giving' that believes it has nothing to receive. What is a closed hand that is unwilling to receive but a fist" (*Circling the Elephant*, 3)

Much of the reflection on the religious traditions of others has historically been focused on simply understanding the neighbor in their difference. There is nothing particularly wrong with that approach, if the goal is simply tolerance and understanding.

But if inter religious learning is "holy labor," as Thatamanil argues, then we need our neighbor's faith and traditions to understand our own.

Perhaps it can be stated this way: I only become a Christian by moving in humility toward my neighbor's wisdom, born out of their religious tradition.

I do not become a Christian by converting them to Christianity. I become a Christian through my own ongoing conversion attempting to love more deeply what my neighbor loves.

Honestly, this should come as no surprise to Christians. Christianity did not emerge wholesale as a complete religion *sui generis*. Christianity is, rather, grounded in Judaism, which was previously shaped by traditions like Zoroastrianism.

Christianity was then shaped by Hellenestic forms of thought and religious practice.

Christianity itself could not and would not be what it is apart from those traditions.

As we now emerge into a 21st century that is more religiously diverse than ever before, we can claim those origins, and as Thatamanil argues, "make it possible for the faithful to conceive of religious diversity as promise rather than problem, as resource rather than as rupture" (29).

He writes,

> One problem in particular captures my attention: the notion that stark and immutable lines separate 'the religions.' Christian reflection has, from its inception, been situated in a world of fluid crosscutting differences. Indeed, it would be possible to craft a history of Christian thought and practice written as a series of interactions with and transmutations of movements and traditions that Christians have come to demarcate as non-Christian. Such a history would demonstrate not only that many of the central categories, practices, and symbols of Christian life are borrowed from Hellenistic philosophical schools, mystery religions, and of course, most vitally from what we now call 'Judaism,' but that for long stretches of history, no clearly defined and rigid boundaries existed between 'Christianity' and those traditions we now take to be Christianity's others (110).

Inter-religious learning has been a hallmark of some of the

most transformative religious movements of our time. Just think of Martin Luther King Jr's leadership of the Civil Rights movement in conversation with Mohandas Gandhi.

Thatamanil asks: "Although it is widely known that King marched alongside and worked with Rabbi Abraham Joshua Heschel and admired the work of Thich Naht Hanh—so much so that he nominated him for the Nobel Peace Prize—why haven't we named this moment as inter religious?" (197).

And this tantalizing point: "What is incontestable is King's claim that Gandhi was the first to demonstrate and embody [a vision of Jesus as engaged in collective nonviolent resistance] on a mass sociopolitical scale and so vindicate any political reading of Jesus that might have been available prior to Gandhi. That a Hindu should be the first to accomplish this revolutionary work is what strikes King as remarkable. To assert the Christianness of Gandhi then is not so much an attempt to baptize him but is instead an act of affirmation that a Hindu understood and performed the true meaning of Jesus's life and teachings more deeply than any Christian had heretofore done" (206).

Christians can practice theological vulnerability. We signal willingness to entertain the possibility that others may be able to shed more light even on our most precious categories than we can manage when left to our own devices.

What if the calling of our time, a calling from the Holy Herself, is to adventure and sojourn into new religious terrain, not now to convert and to conquer as Western Christians once did, but to humbly and hospitably receive other wisdoms?

And intriguingly, might that be the most Trinitarian practice of all?

FOR FURTHER READING

J. Thatamanil, *Circling the Elephant: A Comparative Theology of Religious Diversity*, Fordham University Press, 2020.

14

A SERMON ON THE MOUNT VS. NICENE CREED THROW DOWN

Not every chapter in this guidebook will comment on popular memes, but this chapter does. A graphic Kindle quote from Robin R. Meyers has been making the rounds, and it encapsulates in very brief form a general progressive critique of contemporary Christianity. The meme reads: "Consider this remarkable fact: in the Sermon On the Mount, there is not a single word about what to believe, only words about what to do and how to be. By the time the Nicene Creed is written, only three centuries later, there is not a single word in it about what to do and how to be—only words about what to believe" (from the book *Saving God from Religion: A Minister's Search for Faith in a Skeptical Age*).

The basic outlines of this framing are straightforward: *there was a more original impulse in Christianity, centered in Jesus and his teaching, that was about how to live. Unfortunately, over time, this was co-opted by a religious structure and turned into a doctrine about Jesus as a divine person.*

Often this critique is articulated in the distinction between the gospels and Paul, that Jesus was focused on a way of living whereas Paul was focused on faithfulness to Jesus as Christ. Other times this critique is focused on the rise of Christendom and the problems with Constantine, with Constantine turning Christianity into the state's religion (the most popular and widely read version of this can be found in Dan Brown's *The Da Vinci Code*).

So here's the moment when I tell you I think this whole line of argumentation is misguided. Admittedly, some parts of this thesis are attractive. Like Robin R. Meyers, I have a "high view" of the Sermon on the Mount. And I do think some versions of Christianity hyper-focus on accepting "beliefs" about Jesus to the exclusion of taking Jesus as a moral exemplar.

The problems with the thesis have much more to do with it being historically inaccurate and a poor form of genre criticism. Let us take each of those in turn.

Regarding historical accuracy: even during the historical period when the gospels were being written, Christian communities were concerned *both* with the content of Jesus' teaching *and* with his status as Son of God. A developing doctrine of Jesus as a member of the Trinity is present in the gospels just as much as report about his teachings.

So too at the time the Nicene Creed is getting worked out. Yes, the church was working out a very precise doctrinal creed about who it wanted to say Jesus was and the Trinity was more generally, but it did so at the same time that all those same bishops and theologians were regularly reflecting in their preaching and teaching also on the life of Jesus as a model for Christian living.

The problem with genre criticism: The Sermon on the Mount isn't a creed, it's the report of a sermon contained in a larger text called a gospel. The Nicene Creed isn't a guide to living, it's a creed hammered out in a gathering of church leaders and theologians in order to come to a unified sense of who they all said together God was as Father, Son, and Holy Spirit.

In other words, it's just not a fair comparison, because the person writing Matthew had one goal in mind in what they were writing, and the creed writers had another. Both are single moments within the wider authorship of these people. Neither text totally encapsulates the whole of what they were about.

So here is the counter-thesis. The problem does not lie in the difference between what Matthew was writing in the 70s or 80s A.D. and what the authors of the Nicene Creed were writing in the third century. That's a facile and false distinction that ends up not being fair or helpful.

Instead, the problem inasmuch as there is one, lies first in liturgical usage, and second in a more subtle reframing of how we think about the authority of teachers. Let's take each of these in turn.

On Liturgical Usage: A large part of our problem, which actually can be easily rectified, is that at least in "liturgical" churches, which many if not most progressive churches are, we have a tradition of reciting the creeds, but we don't have a tradition of reciting the Sermon On the Mount.

It's intriguing that, for example, in our Lutheran tradition we recite many aspects of our catechism in worship (the creed, the Lord's Prayer) but we don't recite the Ten Commandments (also contained in the catechism). Why is this? Historically it seems churches have recognized the importance and centrality of the Ten Commandments but never made it liturgical practice to recite them.

This ends up giving the impression in worship that there is more of a focus on naming God than there is on pondering God's commands. However, this is not the fault of the author of the creeds or the author of the commandments, it's really the fault of liturgical planners and how liturgy is constructed.

So, on this point, the insight we can gain from Robin R. Meyers is not so much a denigration of third century Christianity and more an invitation to reform how we worship. We might consider bringing into worship more of the historically canonical texts that help us center the question: how then shall we live?

Top of mind for these kinds of texts would be the Beatitudes, or the prayer of St. Francis, or the Ten Commandments, but also instructive and fascinating, Dorothee Sølle's Credo (included at the conclusion of this chapter because of its length). Faith communities might also consider simply rewriting the creed (many already do this) and include in it more content from Jesus' life and teaching and perhaps also the women disciples and/or the life of Israel with God. An example in the last couple of decades of this happening in another tradition was the Roman Catholic addition in 2002 of the Luminous Mysteries to the praying of the Rosary.

My invitation to readers in this point is to reconsider the assumed superiority Robin R. Meyers and others perhaps unintentionally move us toward when we conclude that somehow the third century Christians co-opted an original and purer form of Christianity. That's a helpful thesis. The point is to focus on our own practice, and to keep in mind every era of faith requires in their moment reform and refocusing.

On the Authority of Teachers: But the other and perhaps more subtle theological issue in all of this has to do indeed with the Sermon on the Mount vs. the Nicene Creed. We can ask, are they really so separate and different? Answer: No.

Take for example a comparison between the "I Have a Dream" speech of Martin Luther King Jr. and his biography. We can't really argue that somehow the dream speech is purer and more original, and the biography too focused on King's life. Instead, we know the "I Have a Dream" sermon has secular power because of who King had become within his culture at that time, and any biography written about him is now written at least in part *because* of the power of his preaching and leadership *and also* as continuing reflection on his authority as a preacher and organizer.

In other words, the content of preaching and the authority

of the preacher go hand in hand. This is an insight that goes back as far as Aristotle in his distinctions between ethos, pathos, and logos. *Ethos* is about the authority of the speaker, *logos* is the word itself, and *pathos* is the role of the audience.

So, in our original examples, it's clear the Sermon on the Mount is the *logos*. It's the word itself, the text of the argument. The Nicene Creed is a post-facto articulation of the *ethos*, attempting to establish the authority of the speaker (Jesus) who spoke things like the Sermon on the Mount.

Finally, the real issue in all of this then is the *pathos*: as an audience, how do we hear and feel about the authority of the speaker and the word the speaker has spoken? Progressive Christians believe the unique thing about Jesus Christ is that his word and his identity are one and the same. For this reason, we should have absolutely no problems confessing the full Nicene Creed any more than we have any problems recognizing the full authority of the Sermon On the Mount, because we believe his authority comes from who he is, because who he is modeled/exemplified the words he spoke. All the creed does (which of course is a lot) is articulate in short form who he is in relationship to God.

Now, having written all of this, we're left with you as the reader deciding whether or not I've made a reasonable argument (logos), whether you trust me as the one to say such things (ethos), and then whether such an argument can sway you given where you are in reflecting on these things (pathos).

Now, have fun with Dorothee Sølle's Credo, which was her incredibly poetic attempt to make the creed a living document in her community as they gathered weekly for Political Even-song. You might even, if you dare, draft a politically charged yet faithfully rendered credo for your own time and context. As Sølle says in her creed, "God desires the counter-argument of the living."

~

CREDO

>*I believe in God*
>*who created the world not ready made*
>*like a thing that must forever stay what it is who does not*
>*govern according to eternal laws that have perpetual validity*
>*nor according to natural orders*
>*of poor and rich,*
>*experts and ignoramuses,*
>*people who dominate and people subjected.*
>*I believe in God*
>*who desires the counter-argument of the living and the alter-ation of every condition*
>*through our work*
>*through our politics.*
>*I believe in Jesus Christ*
>*who was right when he*
>*"as an individual who can't do anything" just like us*
>*worked to alter every condition*
>*and came to grief in so doing*
>*Looking to him I discern*

how our intelligence is crippled,
our imagination suffocates,
and our exertion is in vain
because we do not live as he did
Every day I am afraid
that he died for nothing
because he is buried in our churches, because we have betrayed
his revolution in our obedience to and fear
of the authorities.
I believe in Jesus Christ
who is resurrected into our life
so that we shall be free
from prejudice and presumptuousness from fear and hate
and push his revolution onward
and toward his reign
I believe in the Spirit
who came into the world with Jesus,
in the communion of all peoples
and our responsibility for what will become of our earth: a
valley of tears, hunger, and violence
or the city of God.
I believe in the just peace
that can be created,
in the possibility of meaningful life
for all humankind,
in the future of this world of God.
Amen

15

SALVATION AND CONTROL

The relaxed approach to salvation progressive church takes separates us almost more than anything else from larger western Christian movements. If you want to trigger conservative Christians, one of the easiest methods is to raise the specter of universalism.

Let's go ahead and say it: most progressives are universalists. We tend toward the belief that God is about the work of restoring/healing/making everything whole.

If forced to answer the question "will everyone be saved?" we'll simply go with the affirmative: Yes.

I love what the contrarian Lutheran Søren Kierkegaard wrote in his journals:

> I do not pretend to be better than others. Therefore what the
> old Bishop once said to me is not true–namely, that I spoke as

if the others were going to hell. No, if I can be said to speak at
all of going to hell then I am saying something like this: If the
others are going to hell, then I am going along with them. But I
do not believe that; on the contrary, I believe that we will all be
saved, I, too, and this awakens my deepest wonder.

(*Søren Kierkegaard's Journals and Papers: Autobiographi-
cal, 1848-1855*, p. 557)

I frequently recommend, for those who would like a book-
length meditation on how Scripture has been misinterpreted
repeatedly on the topic of universal salvation, David Bentley
Hart's *That All Shall Be Saved: Heaven, Hell, and Universal
Salvation*. For example, he writes:

> For the earliest Christians, the story of salvation was entirely
> one of rescue, all the way through: the epic of God descending
> into the depths of human estrangement to release his creatures
> from bondage to death, penetrating even into the heart of
> hades to set the captives free and recall his prodigal children
> and restore a broken creation. The sacrifice of Christ was not a
> "ransom" paid to the Father, but rather the "manumission fee"
> (λύτρον, lytron) given to purchase the release of slaves held in
> bondage in death's household.

If a longform approach to this topic interests you, I recommend Bentley Hart's book wholeheartedly. *A Guidebook To
Progressive Church* intentionally remains brief in order to cover
a wide range of topics in short, readable chapters. In the mean-

time, there are a couple of concerns about traditional notions of salvation that we will address in this chapter.

First is the basic presumption, made by many in religious community, that they can know for sure who is saved and who isn't. There's a basic confidence in many communities that if you "get saved"—which in this tradition is defined roughly as accepting Jesus as your personal Lord and Savior following some path of contrition and prayerful acceptance, followed by baptism by immersion—then you can be certain of your salvation. Concomitantly you can also be confident that those who have not been saved like you have been saved are NOT going to be saved, unless they also pray the Jesus prayer and get baptized.

All the others, anyone who wasn't saved like you are, are living under threat. Their eternal salvation is at stake. Believing this, communities become very concerned about getting out into the world to "save the lost," by which they mean "getting people to believe the way they believe." This is why so many of the largest churches are so focused on missions. A ginormous church here in our community has as their mission statement: "Reaching Northwest Arkansas, America, and the World for Jesus Christ."

Those are some big pants.

There are many, many presumptions in such a mission statement, beginning with the notion that the unreached need to be reached, that the unreached are actually "unreached," and that anyone should ever under any circumstances use the word "reaching" in the first place. The presumptions multiply: that the church reaching has something the unreached don't, that no one else has already reached before they reached.

And so on.

Implicit in this kind of mission is a basic paternalism. *We* have something *others* do not. Because they are our subordinates (they are not yet saved whereas we are saved), it is our responsibility, in their best interests, to reach them with this "gospel" we bring. We will restrict and condemn their current practices and beliefs because the message we are bringing to them is, even if they don't know it yet, superior to theirs and in their own best interests. They don't know they aren't saved, but we can fix that. We *must* try to fix that.

A second concern is the presumption that we can actually know who is saved. This is odd, given there is sufficient evidence in Scripture alone to disabuse all Christians of this notion. Scripture is full of texts illustrating how dangerous it is to assume you are saved while others aren't. Just look at Matthew 25, Jesus' parable of the sheep and the goats, where literally everyone is caught by surprise, both those who "inherit the kingdom" and those who don't.

The greatest danger in Christianity, as seen over and over in the history of God with God's people and in the teachings of Jesus, is literally to hold the opinion that you can know that some are saved and others aren't, and you are one of the chosen. The Bible is one giant warning against holding such opinions.

Instead, what we get in Scripture (despite quite a bit of co-optation to the contrary) is the story of God's continuing relating to their people and all of creation with the ultimate promise that all of it will be, in the last day, gathered up into God.

This is why so many progressives are reluctant to spend a lot of time talking about universalism or salvation because it distracts us from the more nuanced and beautiful sense articulated in Scripture of divinization (theosis, deification). Here the Eastern Orthodox and some other Christian traditions (see Irenaeus and Origen and so on) get this much better than most of Western Christianity.

The classic text is 1 Corinthians 15:28, that "God will be all in all," or as the CEV translates it: "Then God will mean everything to everyone."

The full sentence of 1 Corinthians 15:28 reads: "But when all things have been brought under his control, then the Son himself will also be under the control of the one who gave him control over everything so that God may be all in all." There is even in Paul's articulation of God's being "all in all" a kind of structure of "control" we'll need to consider and circle back to. But I like David Bentley Hart on this point:

> But God is not a god, and his final victory, as described in scripture, will consist not merely in his assumption of perfect supremacy "over all," but also in his ultimately being "all in all."

This is closer to what we mean when we say we believe in universalism or that "all will be saved." It is not, and this is crucial, that we believe everyone will end up saying the Jesus prayer and getting baptized even if they haven't yet, or that somehow all peoples and all of creation will be saved in the way we personally envision salvation.

Rather, what we believe (perhaps we should say what we trust) is that God is the sort to make things right. We do not know precisely *how*—and suspect the *what* of salvation to be far more integral and holistic than anything we can imagine—but operate by and large with a considerable degree of trust in God to get it right, ultimately speaking.

Because we live with that basic level of trust, we simply don't concern ourselves overly much with eternal salvation. We're far more interested in, and believe Christian communities are invited to concern themselves with, the ways in which we can live now in greater or lesser resonance with God's ultimately making whole all things.

It makes very little sense to preach a sermon that will convince anyone that if they just believe the right things they'll be saved, if we haven't spoken in a community in a way that inspires that community to meet the basic needs of their neighbors. You might say that neighbor-love in action is the sign of a community who lives in abiding trust of a God who has the whole "salvation" thing under control.

This brings us back around, in the end, to the issue of control. We've just used the word "control" in a surprisingly comfortable manner. To say God has salvation "under control" means, as we say colloquially, "they've got this." It's all good.

"Don't worry, I ordered the cake for the birthday party." That kind of "it's under control."

However, the message of how Jesus has accomplished salvation is often utilized in communities of faith in a way that is attempting an altogether different kind of control. The concept, popular among many Christian communities, is that Jesus offered himself up as a substitution or sacrifice for us. We would have borne God's wrath for our sins, but instead God inflicts all that wrath on his Son Jesus on the cross.

This way of thinking about the cross is very popular in many Christian circles because it gives the leaders of those circles power and control. They can use the threat that somehow if you don't get fully covered in the blood of Jesus, you'll be outside protection from the wrath of God as a way to keep people in community, and control them while they're in it.

You see this all over whenever people are excluded from community once they step outside the strong social controls, if they come out as gay, or get divorced, or start espousing socialist political opinions. It's not just that they are alienated from the community. They also come under threat of God's wrath.

Progressives believe Christ's death on the cross signifies something different. We believe Christ's death on the cross was, very simply, his solidarity with us. Christ was willing to bear the consequences of committing fully to love of neighbor, particularly the poor. All of us are familiar with how difficult it is to truly stand in the breach for the vulnerable. For example, it's rather hard for the executive of a large poultry company to advocate for an actual living wage and protection for workers and a union because they are likely to lose their job.

Jesus was willing to live sacrificially and became a sacrifice, not in the sense of appeasing God's wrath but as simply living authentically in solidarity with the world. And like anyone who does this, as we see time and again, from Martin Luther King Jr. to Archbishop Romero, this can result in death.

However, how this relates to eternal salvation has nothing to do with 'satisfying' God and everything to do with 'solidifying' God. Something shifts in God in terms of God's solidarity. God is now the God who is in Jesus, the Jesus who died on the cross, so whatever our relationship to death was God now also has that relationship with death, and whatever relationship God has with death in Jesus is now the relationship we have with death.

In Christ God overcame death. The promise becomes: we will also. How everything will look the other side of death, we leave that up to God. God's got it under control. We have no interest in using the space created by God conquering death to conquer others. Progressive Christianity does not grasp preaching about eternal salvation as an instrument of control. It instead trusts God and invests in the freedom to love our neighbors, taking the model of Jesus as an icon of how much struggle that will be at times.

If we are going to talk about eternal salvation, that's probably the focus. We'll need the kind of trust we can muster in a God who sees to such salvation to "see us through" living in this world in the way of Jesus's cross.

. . .

FOR FURTHER READING

D. Bentley Hart, *That All Shall Be Saved: Heaven, Hell, and Universal Salvation*, Yale University Press, 2021.

16

WHAT IS IT ABOUT MUSIC?

I'm "mail-ordered-ten-Christian-CDs-for-a-penny" years old. I thought Jars of Clay was the bomb but also, for a time, so were Stryper and DC Talk and Newsboys and Michael W Smith and Amy Grant.

I'm slightly embarrassed by this.

In church on Sunday mornings, I sang from the Lutheran hymnal, and at camp memorized dozens of church camp songs. But for some reason the ubiquity of Christian radio and the popularity of Christian bookstores had me convinced I needed, out of fidelity to my religious heritage, to also follow the Contemporary Christian Music (CCM) charts.

I've always been enough of a completist that when, presented with the challenge to "know" a genre or artist, I lean in.

Along the way I remained fascinated with the few bands

that somehow crossed over between "regular" music and "Christian" music. Somehow, they were clearly and overtly Christian but didn't sell under the moniker CCM.

My favorite was U2 but I also loved King's X and Dolly Parton. Each is their own kind of Christian, all still perform today, all are as far as I know still Christian, but have never taken up the "Christian" label.

I think what broke me of the CCM habit was a MercyMe concert in Wisconsin in the Aughts: the singer said something along the lines of how the band that opened for them was "reaching the culture" for Jesus.

I don't remember who opened for them. I do remember that line, and how much it chafed.

I started drifting toward bands that were weirdly Christian. I fell in love for a time with a lot of the bands recording with Asthmatic Kitty Records, bands like The Welcome Wagon and Half-Handed Cloud and most famous of all, Sufjan Stevens, who I will return to later.

Somewhere during that era I spent a bunch of time watching movies and videos made by the Danielson Familie band, which are just about as weird as anything the Oklahoma City natives The Flaming Lips put out, but cuter. I also listened to some of the indie (and admittedly niche) Lutheran musicians like Jonathan Rundman and Nate Houge and Rachel Kurtz and David Scherer.

I guess all of this was in that long late phase when people still bought CDs. But when Spotify emerged, slowly my passion for weird indie waned somewhat. I still love Yankee Hotel

Foxtrot (which I believe epitomizes that era and genre of indie) but like Wilco I've retreated from the more "precious" aspects of that sound. Mileage may vary.

All of this leaves me wondering how we choose the music we choose and why. Clearly some of my listening habits have emerged based on a desire for identity markers at the intersection of indie and Christian.

More and more I just listen to music I like, by anyone and with a drastically ecumenical comportment toward faith(s), and I think that's how the vast majority of listeners function.

This whole reflection was spurred because a couple of weeks ago our children's ministry leader sent me some recordings of Natalie Bergman. She wants to sing some of her songs with our children's choir.

I did what I typically do with new musicians, I looked up and read her bio on Spotify. Turns out she was part of a duo, Wild Belle, that was popular during the heyday of indie.

I wanted to figure out where her Christian impulse came from. I'll admit, I've got levels of suspicion I can't shake, post-MercyMe concert. Was it strategic, "trying to reach the culture?" That's a basic suspicion of Christian musicians I can't shake.

But Bergman, like some other recent musicians (think M.I.A.) had a conversion experience that resulted in a musical reckoning. In this sense her move toward singing Christian songs is existential and careful rather than strategic or missional.

In a recent interview with J.L. Sirisuk for example:

JLS: Why did you want to make this a gospel record – what's your relationship with gospel music?

NB: Well, lets see. I don't even know if it's appropriate to call the music gospel because gospel traditionally comes from black churches, but I do think that it was inspired by traditional gospel music and also Christian music. I'm not that into Christian radio – some of the music is a little cheesy, but I just wanted to have my own interpretation of the gospels. I wasn't afraid to sing about Jesus, but it is a hard time to be a Christian in America right now, or anywhere really because religion has such a bad name. Historically some people have done some horrible things in the name of God, and I don't know where it went wrong but I would say I'm a Christian fighting the good fight and I want that to be the message. I want the message to be love and the goodness of the creator and why we were created. I think the message got a little bit skewed somewhere along the lines and people are just taking religion and corrupting it. I thought that singing gospel music was the appropriate thing to do ('The gospel of Natalie Bergman: accepting loss through God, love and music,' J.L. Sirisuk, *Hero*, March 5, 2021).

This is evocative of a highly idiosyncratic album. I've loved

Rickie Lee Jones' "the sermon on exposition boulevard", which is what I guess I'd call Christian adjacent.

It's Christian but with an authentic connection to the heart of that particular music, and faithful in the sense that it emerges not in order to accomplish something else (convert people) but simply to express that which the artist feels called to express (which can and often is about faith).

I love this kind of thing.

I know, I'm probably supposed to like some of the older Christian music. The stuff written back when almost all music was religious music. And I've gone through phases when I enjoyed listening to Bach, or Gregorian chant, etc.

But again, I mostly listen to what I like, and what I like these days is seldom overtly Christian... except when it is.

I'm reminded of the phase I went through about a decade ago, when I was totally into Olivier Messiaen. He was a devout Christian and served at Église de la Sainte-Trinité, Paris, where he was titular organist for 61 years.

But he also famously composed much of his music as evocation of bird song. Somehow this makes sense to me, and I love the bird music even more than the organ music.

As a friend recently wrote, "Likewise the whole of Creation sings a harmonious song. Most people agree with this logic, but don't notice on a typical day, except for a day like we experienced during the eclipse, when its absence was felt. Birdsong changed when darkness fell. When we learn to view all of Creation as the Church, then we will truly be United, One.”

I promised I'd return to Sufjan Stevens. Even if you don't recognize the name, you've probably heard some of his Christmas songs during the holidays, as his Christmas albums are incredibly popular (and lovely). Sojourners recently published a piece about Stevens and his new album, Javelin.

The title is wonderful: 'The Queer Christian Yearning of Sufjan Stevens'. Ezra Craker the interviewer, writes:

> Sufjan's songs exemplify just the kind of dramatic, earnest yearning that works on people like my friend and me: queer, raised Christian, and unlucky in love at practically every turn. Locked out of traditional paths to partnership, especially in the communities we come from, we search for a love that can hold our whole selves—faith, queerness, and all.
>
> Stevens has been an expert in this kind of longing since he started releasing experimental indie music in the early 2000s. He has sung about his search for both divine and human love with equal depth and specificity, often making it difficult to distinguish between the two.

Even Stevens himself, with some of his recent albums, has wandered from the more precious indie rock of his earlier period and into the creation of ambient music (like Trent

Reznor, but nicer). I like to imagine he's on a similar musical and spiritual journey as many of us. But on Javelin, he once again leans into this crossover theological approach that is secular and sacred precisely in its queerness, and as a listener it's like circling back around to all those albums of the mail-order era, but now I can like and trust it, because as Craker points out, "Stevens' music has never been either gay or about God. It's indivisibly gay *and* about God."

If we are going to talk about music, I would be remiss not to offer some real talk about the specific musical tradition in which I was raised. I imagine the average newcomer to our church finds some of what we sing in worship surprising, new, difficult, even foreign. This has so much to do with denominational history and the many and varied ways Christian groups have cultivated their musical heritage, so I tell you this story here as just one example.

I grew up participating in Sunday worship that followed the order of worship from the Lutheran Book of Worship (LBW), a thick green hymnal that populated each pew of the church, hand-made bookmarks dangling from the spine and tickling our knees as we sidled into our spots each week.

The LBW was the work of an "Inter-Lutheran Commission on Worship," inclusive of Lutherans in North America. It was developed at the same time the ecumenical liturgical renewal was happening among neighboring traditions and turned out to be a dynamic and sturdy hymnal, remaining as the hymnal of our denomination for almost 30 years.

The ecumenical context for its development was formative. Philip H. Pfatteicher writes,

> The work of the Second Vatican Council had its effect on the Anglican world as well. As Lutherans began work on their book, Episcopalians were working on a revision of the American Book of Common Prayer, continuing its distinctive traditions and making use of the emerging work of the Roman church. There was therefore a remarkable convergence of the effort of three Christian bodies, and the Lutherans were the beneficiaries of the work of the Roman Catholics as well as of the Episcopalians. Lutherans were moving out of the confines of their own traditions and learning to open their eyes to other traditions and practices to the enrichment of their own life and worship.

What we had in our hands when we worshipped was an order of worship inspired by developments in increasingly ecumenical liturgies but with music specifically written by 1970s Lutheran composers. The book contained three "settings" of the liturgy, plus about 500 hymns and a bunch of other attendant resources (prayers, the Psalms, orders of service for special occasions like private confession, baptism, weddings and funerals, etc.). One of my seminary professors frequently mentioned when he participated in selecting those 500 hymns for the hymnal, they started with a stack of over 10,000 hymns suggested by members of the denomination. Printed out, the stack was almost as tall as he was.

By the time I was about ten, I think I had entirely memorized all three of those settings. I only needed the hymnal for the hymns, I could sing and pray all the other content because I knew it by heart. I still do.

I also learned through repetition that what counts as "worship" is to walk procedurally through various portions of a liturgy, a formalized movement that begins with an entrance rite, settles into the word and preaching, gathers the community for a meal, and then sends them out into "the world."

I now pastor in Arkansas, a location at some distance from the Lutheran heartland, and many, if not most, worshippers in our church know little of the history of the development of these ecumenical liturgies. Even the liturgy itself is strange to many. It takes quite a lot of explanation. Many in our community come from non-liturgical traditions, church movements that host more loosely structured praise song services centering a long sermon (in worship studies this style of worship has sometimes been called "Frontier Worship" because it developed in early America on the "frontiers"). Most of these churches do not recite prayers or litanies or creeds. In fact, some traditions are quite skeptical of such "rote" liturgy and avoid doing it.

There are widely differing views on how to pray "from the heart." For the liturgical, more textual traditions, we may memorize prayers to pray them by heart. For the non-liturgical types, we may prefer to lift in our prayers what comes to mind in the moment, lifting what is currently "on our heart." What

I've always valued about the rote parts of the service is the rote-ness. This is most clearly illustrated in the praying of the Lord's Prayer. It is the one memorized prayer still reliably inscribed into the neurons of almost all those gathered for weddings, funerals, and other solemn occasions. Because everyone has memorized it, it need not be printed or explained, but can simply be "done."

But what is the path for bringing anything new into the collective consciousness and memory of a people? For those of us tasked with designing our liturgies, what's difficult is knowing how and when to bring something new into the community's liturgy and then repeat it frequently enough that it becomes rote.

There is a kind of journey the community collectively goes on to learn something new. For example, when I arrived at my current call (where I've now served for fourteen years), relatively soon I introduced Jonathan Rundman's *Heartland Liturgy* into the contemporary service repertoire. At first, it was very new, and new in multiple ways. Rundman's liturgy is a (theo-logically progressive) "rock" liturgy, but it also follows the struc-ture of the ecumenical liturgies. Rundman is a Lutheran rock musician, and he intentionally composed music (innovative then and still) in a contemporary style that conformed to the texts and structure of the "ordo."

What would an exercise in developing a liturgy that is "of the people" mean? Forget about the divide between those who like liturgy that is rote vs. those who like liturgy that is sponta-neous. I'm interested in the actual "heart" of liturgy, why we do what we do or why we even do it in the first place. This would be truly progressive liturgy and would require sensitivity to the actual history of communal worship combined with nimble, responsive openness to the needs and makeup of the people.

What is new to a community singing the *Heartland Liturgy* is both the music AND the structure. Part of this is how the songs are made up (for example, the Kyrie and Hymn of Praise in our tradition offer a call and response pattern), and part of it is in the structure of the service as a whole (the liturgy moves from Word to Sacrament weekly and includes musical components for each of the steps for these, such as a musical introit for the Psalms and an entire liturgy for the distribution of communion).

Our congregation has now been singing the *Heartland Liturgy* for many years (off and on, because we do rotate other settings in and out depending on the season). We know it "by heart." But we only know it by heart because we've been willing to take the risk of praying it each week, week after week, for years. What once felt distant or strange now feels close and familiar.

However, we still don't know the liturgy by heart in the way a large group of Swifties knows Taylor Swift's repertoire. This is likely because most Christians in our community do not pull up liturgical music and listen to it on repeat in their cars and before bed or while working out. I always find it a fascinating comparison, how willing groups of humans are to learn all the songs of a particular musician, while reserving the music of worship only for the sporadic times they gather Sundays for worship. I believe this means some aspects of what humans have always considered "worship" have transitioned into secular spaces. It's why we go to concerts.

What's fascinating about a large crowd all singing along in unison is what it represents. When a crowd can all sing the same songs from memory, it signifies not only that they know the songs, but that they are part of a group, a collective. When churches are full of people who primarily listen but don't sing along to the liturgy, I think it means they don't identify (on some deeper level) in quite the same way fans identify with one another in fan culture.

In 2006 our denomination published a hymnal to replace the LBW. They went back to the cranberry color (also the color of the '60s era hymnal that preceded the LBW) and called the new volume Evangelical Lutheran Worship (ELW). One difference that came with this new hymnal was a shift in philosophy: the hymnal, rather than attempting to be comprehensive (one book, one people), containing everything we would or could sing and pray in worship, instead served as the core of a set of liturgical resources published by the denomination. Over time our publishing house has published a wonderful proliferation of extra volumes (including new volumes for the pews like the ecological social justice themed All Creation Sings) available for worship, and an entire repository online we can access for even more resources. The denomination has also published specifically ethnic hymnals *This Far By Faith*, an African-American resource, and *Libro de Liturgia y Cántico*.

This means when you sit down in our pews, depending on

where you worship, you now have over 1000 hymns available in the pew, and yet those thousand songs are not the "complete set" but rather the core for a wider set of options (and I have not even mentioned the music we began this chapter with, all the popular Contemporary Christian Music).

Options are the name of the game. Just like you can order thousands of drink combinations at Starbucks, so too the options for assembling an order of Christian worship are almost endless. The new hymnal we have been using for the last decade included not three but TEN settings of the liturgy, representing hymnody from the global church, many styles and traditions, and from the now very long tradition of Christian hymnody. Like trying to pick what to listen to next on Spotify, what we are presented with in worship today is both richly varied *and* invokes a kind of decision freeze emerging out of an over-whelming surplus of options.

Even if someone is incredibly faithful in attending worship every single week, even if they take the hymnal home and prac-tice some of the hymns at their guitar or piano, even if they sing them at other assemblies or before or after their meals, the reality is that the repertoire is so extensive, it's hard to know how they could know by heart much of what we do each week. This is the struggle progressive churches face as much as any other church: sing *Amazing Grace* every week on repeat because everyone knows it or introduce new (and more theologically progressive hymns) each week and watch the congregation struggle to learn them.

Liturgy is kind of like the tip of an iceberg, the visible part of a much larger sustaining structure. In our modern moment, it seems that the entirety of Christian worship resources are potentially available at our fingertips. If liturgy is still an iceberg at all, it has been incredibly thinned, more like the thin ice over a newly freezing pond. No one feels the water, they only skate on the ice.

Richard Niebuhr once said that "religious traditions are in permanent revolution." I think what I have described as the shift that has occurred in Lutheran worship, this adoption of an ecumenical liturgy while also proliferating options, has created a situation in which our religious tradition cannot truly experience revolution because all the options are on the table. Yet it simultaneously crowds out all the other "options" that don't go in a hymnal (think of things like the Quaker practice of silence, the activities and actions that make up some Pentecostal services, and really all the widely varied actions that take place in worship that simply don't translate well into a book). It's kind of like neoliberalism's co-optation of everything: the new way of doing liturgy can encompass anything, and therefore risks substantiating nothing.

I know I can't take everyone back to what I remember nostalgically as those wonderful days in my early life when the liturgy was always reliably the same week after week. I like '70s music as much as anyone, but I do recognize life has continued to happen since.

What I do wonder, however, is what it means to focus more carefully on what we think we are doing when we worship these days. I've written this entire chapter about music and the liturgy because that is what I was trained to primarily consider when planning worship. Lutherans love their books. But I've become far more curious as to what an exercise in developing a liturgy that is "of the people" might mean. I think this is the progressive church question that causes me as a worship planner continuing struggle and may at times leave those joining our worship services feeling nonplussed and intrigued simultaneously.

Claudio Carvalhaes in *Liturgies From Below* argues that liturgy is "an invitation to resist the temptation to be co-opted by the Empire, and [to find] the nerve to come out of the Empire, creating counter-imperial alternatives." That's a wonderful theological invitation and also challenging to translate into the actual selection and creation of music and liturgy.

If we were to begin the work today, asking ourselves not what will be in the next hymnal, or how to further broaden a "set of resources" for worship today, what would it mean to host liturgy that resists empire and creates counter-imperial alternatives? That's the step that comes after recognizing the history we have traveled, as well as a crucial filter we can implement to ask ourselves whether we will continue to use this or that hymn.

FOR FURTHER READING
D. Byrne, *How Music Works*, McSweeney's, 2012.

HOW SACRED ARE SACRED
TEXTS?

Sometimes when people come to our congregation they'll say, "You know I was part of this general spiritual community and it was fine, but I just kept needing a bit more Jesus." I think this is their recognition that although as a community we are radically open to traditions not our own, and practice interfaith engagement with many of them (from Hindu to Buddhist to Jewish to Muslim), in the end we are able to practice this engagement gently and faithfully because we are grounded in our own tradition, which really does maintain "a bit more Jesus."

The way most Christian communities keep a bit more Jesus is by keeping a bit more Bible. In other words, although some people may read Harry Potter as a sacred text, or The Odyssey as a sacred text; and although even we in our own tradition will engage the Bible with many of the same tools we are willing to apply to the reading of great works; in the end, we still do believe there is something special about the Bible, and we believe this because we believe in some ways it uniquely helps us encounter Jesus.

This is to say, although some progressive Christians may disagree on this point, progressives have a rather high view of the Bible. It's the main text we read and interpret in worship, it's the source and norm of who we are as a community of faith, and it is, as Luther liked to say, "the cradle in which Christ is lain."

It's important to make the distinction, though, that the Bible isn't Christ. The Bible is the cradle. This is the key hermeneutical insight that distinguishes a liberal reading of Scripture from a fundamentalist one.

How we interpret our sacred Scriptures (hermeneutics) matters quite a lot. I served a congregation in Wisconsin for six years that owned two lovely and historic church buildings. The Norwegian Lutherans had split in the mid-1890s over what was at the time a huge issue—single vs. double predestination. As a result of the split, two beautiful rural churches were built two hundred yards apart from each other on adjacent sides of the cemetery.

Prior to the predestination controversy, Norwegian Lutherans had been split over whether the Bible condoned slavery. One group believed since it is not expressly condemned, it is condoned. Another group believed the overall arc of Scripture indicated condemnation of slavery. Each group read the same Scriptures, but in different ways, and came to fundamentally different conclusions based on the same text.

At the root of both controversies were differing interpretive strategies. One approach assumes that the text, and our interpretation of the text, are essentially the same thing. The other approach cultivates a greater awareness that there might be a much wider chasm between the text and our interpretation of the text.

Simmering underneath almost all controversies—whether they are religious or political ones—are differences in how we interpret, and these two ways of interpreting—painting with a somewhat broad brush here—often become the sides of our bipartisan fallings out.

The fancy word for all of this is hermeneutics, the science of interpretive studies. Hermeneutics recognizes that how we interpret matters. Even more importantly, it recognizes that our lack of awareness of differing approaches to interpretation underlines and reinforces many of our cultural and religious differences.

There is a rather simple way to illustrate the two ways of holding Scripture. The first way is to grip the text tightly. In this approach, the interpreter believes they understand and grasp the text well. How they interpret it is exactly what the text means. This group of readers tends to say things like, "You know as well as I do that the Bible says..." or "The Bible says it, I believe it, that settles it."

The other way to hold Scripture is to hold it lightly. In this approach, the interpreter seeks an understanding of the text, but honors the fact that there are many stages of interpretation between what the text originally says and what the interpreter comes to understand as the meaning of the text. At the very least, with most texts, there are at least these stages—the author, the text, the translation of the text, the reading of the text, the reader, and the reader's ultimate application of the text as it relates to life in the world.

Those are a lot of stages, and because the process is so much more complicated than is often recognized, the interpreter who holds Scripture lightly opts to submit to the truth they hope they are discovering in the text without assuming that they have come to the final and settled single and best interpretation. To hold a text lightly is to keep our eyes open to this complex and beautiful interpretive process.

Consider the Psalms. These beautiful songs and prayers can and have been read any number of ways. One popular approach is to read the Psalms as if we are joining Christ in his prayer. There is some indication this is an appropriate Christian reading of the Psalms, because Christ himself often quotes the Psalms (My God, My God, why have you forsaken me—Psalm 22), and the New Testament quotes the Psalms regularly as well.

As a Christian reader of the Psalms, it makes quite a lot of sense to read the psalms in this way. In fact, it aids praying passages that seem inappropriate to pray otherwise. Joining Christ in Christ's prayer gives us confidence and brings to greater recognition the community of prayer we join whenever we pray them.

However, the Psalms are Scripture we share with other faiths. Reading the Psalms with communities of faith other than our own, we need a different set of tools, another way of reading the psalms, that still makes sense as shared song to God. We can keep our Christological reading of the Scripture for our own devotion and prayer. We can even share this Christological reading of the Psalms with our neighbors of other faiths. But we can only do so lightly, gently, palm up and hand open, entrusting our own way of reading Scripture to the wider community of readers of the text.

When we read the Bible in this way, it makes the reading of Christian Scripture more attractive. We can try to bring this same hermeneutic to bear in every conversation we have with others about Scripture. When we look at a text together, if you say to me, "The Bible obviously says... (insert here any number of hot button topics we currently argue about)," I am going to say, "Let's see if it really says that. What's the wider context? What kinds of cultural assumptions do we bring to the text? Is this a loving interpretation of the text, even if you think it is the 'right' interpretation of the text?"

Think about the different ways you have seen people present something of beauty to you. When they grasp it, Gollum-like, calling it precious and clasping it as their own, do you find it desirable? Do you really think people love and trust the things they squeeze and grasp tightly?

Or if they bring something of beauty to you, gently and lovingly, like a newly discovered kitten, does another and better string play on your heart? Can you see their care of that beautiful thing, their life committed to it, in their gentle open hands?

We hold the Scriptures lightly for the same reason we hold the hands of our family members lightly. Because we love them.

FOR FURTHER READING

J. Caputo's *Hermeneutics: Fact and Interpretation In the Age of Information*, Pelican, 2018.

PART IV

INTERSECTIONS

18

WOMEN'S WORK

A couple of weeks back I shared a popular *Atlantic* article about the decline in church attendance with our church council. The next day our church administrator said to me, "You know what's missing from that *Atlantic* article? Women's work!"

I'll admit to a certain level of blindness on this front. I'm a man and so I always must be intentional, or be called out, so as not to overlook the issue of gender in institutional contexts.

I'm also a progressive, and progressives, for all that they in fact do focus on gender issues, tend to do so at the front edge of what I guess we'd call "third wave" feminism, prioritizing issues of trans-feminism, intersectionality, sex positivity, etc.

We're collectively guilty, I think, of having blown past the first few waves of feminism, assuming erroneously those are passé or fully addressed, when in fact they are not. Not at all.

But not all prognosticators on church-life post-pandemic are as blind to the impact of women's work on the shifts in church culture as that *Atlantic* article. Eileen Campbell-Reed published the #PandemicPastoringReport in 2022, surveying a broad cross-section of church leadership across the U.S., and in her report, a top finding among findings like "recognize that things have changed" and "embrace hybrid options" was this one:

Listen to women.

In 'Research-based guidelines for leading the church in a new era of ministry' (faithandleadership.com), she writes,

> Churches and medical chaplaincy have lost women's leadership in the last three years. Globally, 54 million women stepped out of the workforce in 2020 alone. Stories from my research point out how churches continue to harbor unfair expectations for parents, especially mothers. During the lockdown, untold millions of mothers juggled home-schooling, elder care, and meal and household management—and still did their paying jobs, including ministry. Churches need to reengage women's leadership, listen to the reasons they departed, and envision ways to make ministry more sustainable.

In our local progressive congregation, even though our collective nostalgia for the ways church "used-to-be" may impact how we feel about church life today, and our assumptions about how the institution of church should be shaped is certainly impacted by the embodied memory of how many churches in our culture have functioned, nevertheless if we're really honest and clear about the why and how of church, it's because of women's work.

Funeral luncheons.

Altar guild.

Quilting.

Sunday school.

Bulletin folding.

I can still remember when serving at rural parishes in Minnesota and Wisconsin in the 90s and aughts the three biggest attendance Sundays of the church year: Christmas, Easter, and ... Mother's Day. Because all the grandmas and mothers would ask their otherwise reluctant family members to attend church with them in honor of the day.

I raise this issue not because I've entirely succeeded at an equalitarian relationship in my own marriage. We are still always noticing the many ways in which even when I'm trying to do my part in our aim for equality, nevertheless there are parts of women's work my spouse simply notices better, stewards more carefully, does the labor. There's still a basic inequality in "recognition" for the times when I pick up what would normally be women's work. I get congratulated, whereas if my spouse does it it's simply assumed that's what a woman does.

Now, take all of this and think about it in the church context. Women were the driving force of the church (and church growth) in the 20th century. They had the babies (most church growth last century was related to birth rates). They took the family to church (even if the dads drove). They were the main volunteer force (except for the few roles in church spaces that were the male responsibilities).

Then think about everything that has shifted since that era. Almost all women work now. Very few stay home. Many mothers are single and have primary responsibility for the kids. Many women have taken up the roles reserved for men last century—serving on non-profit boards, getting elected to public office, writing books, podcasting, etc.

How could this shift not starkly impact the life of the church? How could it not be related to church decline? And if we truly believe that women gaining equality with men is "progress," then if church changes as a result of that progress why do we construe it as "decline"?

This was a huge "aha" moment for me as a pastor, and I'm sorry to everyone for being so slow. I've been yearning for a return to church, for movement building. I deeply desire for progressive Christians to know one another, to advocate and strive together in the way of Jesus.

I haven't at all adequately accounted for the reality that calls for the church to "return" to the level of participation we saw last century is essentially regressive. It ignores the progress women have made.

It's also then not surprising at all that many conservative churches are fighting tooth and nail to take us back to "traditional" gender roles, because not only is it a way to control women, it's also a way to maintain the energizing pool of volunteers they need to do "church the way it's always been."

One additional observation: for some time now, I've

pondered the aging of mainline Protestant churches. Back in 2016, the median age of the ELCA was 58, whereas the median age of the country as a whole was 39. I'm assuming this means we're closer to a median of 65 today.

In other words, most ELCA members are retired. The make-up of many comparable churches in our denomination is retired couples who, at least theoretically, have some of the same kind of availability a stay-at-home parent would have had during the 20th century.

What this means for our church is not only the struggle of whether or not to compare ourselves to how church used to be, but also the comparison with how churches are today in a mostly retired denomination.

Our church is not (retired, that is). And it would be a tremendous mismatch to try and do church today in ways that ignore the fact that we are a young congregation and most of the women live a shape-of-life profoundly impacted by the progress of first and second wave feminism (even if admittedly a lot of the gender justice we prioritize is shaped more by third-wave issues).

People are really busy, women in particular, often busy with volunteer service not all of which is done in the church space. That's the reality.

What does this mean in practice? Well, a couple of examples:

- We decided to cater Easter breakfast this year. An Easter brunch potluck style relies on already busy people (mostly women) cooking an egg bake on top of preparing meals for later in the day while also grading all the papers students turned in at the university on Friday.

- We started wondering if, in addition to recruiting people to speak at municipal meetings on justice topics if perhaps we need to provide childcare at the church to free up other voices to go.
- So many families parent in blended or single families. Is our weekly worship schedule accommodating of the attendance patterns and needs of those households?
- Do we even name the realities I'm addressing here in this post? Is it talked about from the pulpit? Are we working to make sure we don't analyze church shifts in ways that layer on the guilt?

This weekend our church council will gather in retreat to vision. It's become clear to me that whatever we imagine as our way of living out of the kin-dom (dropping the "g" because I love how kin-dom reads as a replacement for kingdom) of God together, we need to do more than say that women's work and the shifts in it underlie our thinking.

As Jessica McClard (our church administrator and the founder of the Little Free Pantry movement) points out, "churches don't pursue justice issue advocacy like high quality, affordable child and elder care, equal pay, maternity leave, etc. to say nothing of reproductive justice. It's not so much even a lack of advocacy. It's a lack of acknowledgment that those things are real problems."

We need to shape the life of the church in ways that celebrate and embrace the shifts in gender roles and align ourselves in solidarity (both through advocacy and acknowledgement) with women. It will take some work, especially keeping such work in relationship with the insights we have gained in moving beyond traditional binaries, but isn't that the whole point of progressive church, to discover the gospel-centered intersections that help bring to greater integration things like third and first wave feminism?

FOR FURTHER READING
H. Neumark, *Breathing Space: A Spiritual Journey in the South Bronx*, Beacon Press, 2012

19

NEURODIVERSITY

There's a sensory room at our church, a little place to get away with lower light, plush chairs, a small library, and some sensory toys.

I've had parishioners remark on the gentle, atypical tenor of our worship services, open for "disruptions," the kinds of moments less typical in contexts that expect neurotypical conformity.

Neurodivergent parishioners lead or serve in all aspects of our congregational ministry, and I think it's very likely some of our most unique, transformative ministries have come about precisely because neurodivergence operates as an embodied, spiritual gift.

This isn't at all to say that we're completely "there," as if everything we do is already fully informed by the insights of neurodiversity advocacy. Quite to the contrary, I think intentionally patterning church life with neurodiversity in mind is a growth area for us. Some of our main programs like Queer Camp are ahead of the curve. But, for example, I'm still trying to figure out how to manage the different needs of worshippers, some who want the organ to rumble their very bones and others for whom the volume of the organ or band makes the sanctuary unwelcoming.

But if we are not yet there, we are at least aware, and growing in our awareness. It's been remarkable hearing from parishioners who are diagnosed as autistic as adults. It's a real "aha!" moment, because it helps the one with the diagnosis, and their community, understand better who they are as a person and what diverse gifts and needs they bring to the community.

Some of our best steps in terms of welcoming neurodivergency as a part of Christian life come naturally, as if we were born to it—because I guess we were. But in the same way that heteronormativity and other kinds of cultural norms dominate in many spaces, so too we are always in the process of overcoming to explore what it means to truly be a diverse people of God.

The summer we started Queer Camp (a week-long camp for LGBTQIA+ youth), I finally had the chance to watch *Crip Camp*, a documentary about the disability revolution. That film documents a remarkable moment: a camp for teens facing disabilities is founded in the woods of the Catskill Mountains, and out of the bonds formed at that camp arose a revolution that became the Disability Rights Movement.

I've often thought perhaps queer teen youth programs like Queer Camp may serve a similar and pivotal role. Who knows what kind of revolution can happen when queer youth find each other, build connections, and dream.

There is considerable overlap between queer advocacy, disability advocacy, and neurodivergent advocacy. The communities are intertwined in many ways. I think I first came to an awareness of the extent of this reality when I read *Care Work: Dreaming Disability Justice* by Leah Lakshmi Piepzna-Samarasinha, a book about "creating spaces by and for sick and disabled queer people of colour, and creative "collective access"—access not as a chore but as a collective responsibility and pleasure—in our communities and political movements."

Whenever I read a book like this, I think to myself, "Why didn't someone in the church write this?" Then I ask myself, "Why do I want a Christian book on this topic?" And then I tell myself, "Actually, you don't. It's probably better it isn't."

Nevertheless, the spirit of the book is the spirit I wish to inhabit and spend time with. In that sense, and this is a common phenomenon in my life, I find that Leah Lakshmi Piepzna-Samarasinha's work is more "faithful" than a lot that passes as religious reflection on neurodivergency. I recommend it highly.

There has been considerably more literature produced at the intersection of disability and theology than neurodiversity. A recent example is the widely acclaimed *My Body is Not a Prayer Request: Disability Justice In the Church* by Amy Kenny. Put "disability and theology" as search terms in an Amazon search and you'll see what I mean.

My theory on why this is the case is twofold. First, because Christianity is indeed focused on "the body," and because the Disability Rights Movement in the 1960s and 70s enlivened the minds of many theologians of that generation, we have seen the fruits of that work in the academy and church (even if they haven't been widely applied). But the conversation around and insights into neurodiversity are more recently won and ongoing, so it should come as no surprise that studies of neurodiversity and theology are still forthcoming.

Also, the mind is even more complex than the body, so perhaps it is harder for writers to get their "minds" around the issues.

We can take our lead, per usual, from neurodiverse people themselves. It's a worthwhile exercise in church community to sit down with those who have sensory processing needs, or are autistic or neurodiverse in some other way, and find out what barriers there are to full participation in the life of the church, but also what gifts they bring that can crack open some of the old complacencies of neurotypical church.

For further reading, check out Samuel Wells in *The Christian Century*, who reports on attending a conference on theology and neurodiversity, "the first of its kind," in 2020! He concludes with a zinger of a line, "Perhaps neurodiversity could show us the face of God like never before." Perhaps indeed.

FOR FURTHER READING

L. Piepzna-Samarasinha, *Care Work: Dreaming Disability Justice*, Arsenal Pulp Press, 2018.

QUEERING CHRISTIANITY

One of the accusations frequently leveled against progressive Christians by other Christians is that we are simply conforming to this world rather than being transformed by the gospel of Christ.

So quite a lot of our communication is rearguard action, trying to defend against such critique. People will say, for example, "You welcome gay people at your church, but that doesn't mean you approve of their lifestyle, right?"

There's a lot loaded into such questions. Approve... Lifestyle... Lots of assumptions, lots of judgment. In fact, those who ask such questions seem to be completely unaware of the ways they are being conformed to the thought patterns of this world rather than the freeing gospel of Christ.

That's not counter-blaming. It's just trying to draw attention to what otherwise is overlooked by all the Christians (of whom there are legion) who think they are just "following the Word of God," as if you can access the Word of God purely rather than through your experience and worldview.

Here's the thing: being queer isn't a sin. Your orientation and gender identity are simply part of who you are.

You are created in the image of God, and God says of God's creation, this is very good.

If you've never had the chance, I recommend reading *Queer Virtue: What LGBTQ People Know About Life and Love and How It Can Revitalize Christianity*, by Liz Edman.

Why? Here's the argument. We don't just *tolerate* queer people in our community. Nor do we live as progressive Christians and fully *welcome* them. No, we are being transformed by the virtues they share with us. Our Christianity is queer.

Contra some Christians who believe that progressive Christianity is conformed to this world, we hold that it is traditional Christianity that has been conformed to the binary, oppressive understandings of sexuality, race, and many other things, and needs to be transformed by the queerness of Christ.

If this intrigues you, if you'd like to learn how the virtues of the queer community help identity the virtues present in Christian Scripture and tradition, then you want to read Edman's book.

In part I of her book, Edman walks the reader through the experience of identifying queer virtue. It's about identity, risk, touch, scandal, and adoption.

In part II, she talks about a priestly people (she herself is a gay priest), and identifies what she believes are marks of a priestly people we can learn from the queer community: Pride, Coming Out, Authenticity, and Hospitality.

For Edman, *queerness is not just compatible with Christianity, but is an embodiment of it.*

For Edman, *authentic Christianity is a spiritual journey that prioritizes the ancient Christian impulse to rupture simplistic binaries, especially those pertaining to the relationship between Self and Other* (xiii.).

Edman argues that *queer ethical demands clearly and often exquisitely manifest widely recognized Christian virtues: spiritual discernment, rigorous self-assessment, honesty, courage, material risk, dedication to community life, and care for the marginalized and oppressed.*

She writes,

> For too long, public discourse about LGBTQ people has tended to operate from the premise that queer identity is morally problematic, but that there are specific instances of individual queer people who live upright lives. I argue precisely the opposite: while individual queer people struggle at times with moral failing–as all human beings do–in general I perceive queer identity to have at its core a moral center of high caliber, one that is both inspirational and aspirational. My experience being immersed in the lives of and spiritual journeying of queer people tells me plainly not only that the divine is alive and well in us, but that many of us are deeply attuned to it.

In her chapter on coming out she offers this challenge to progressive Christians:

Maybe you are already living the liberating strand of Christianity. Maybe you have found it in a vibrant, friendly church that treats kids well and has a nice cluster of gay people in regular attendance. That's great, truly. But understand this: our faith tells us that it isn't enough to believe it quietly, to go to church on Sunday with less fanfare than you might go to brunch, or to the grocery store. You have to explain to people what you are doing, and why it matters to you. What you are feeling, perceiving, and perhaps living out in community with others is caught up in what Jesus called 'the good news,' and it matters very much that you tell other people about it.

The most important thing that progressive Christians can do to advance an accurate understanding of our faith is to come out as a Christian. And specifically, to come out as the kind of Christian you truly are.

The necessity of coming out is one of those basic things that progressive Christians should be learning from queer people. When you know who you are and what you are about, it matters to tell people about it. But listen up, all you shy Christians out there: queer people know something that you may not know. WE KNOW HOW TO DO THAT.

Begin by getting in touch with your own identity, with Pride. Coming out is first and foremost a conversation that is about you. This matters to understand: you aren't coming out to people in order to change them. Hopefully you are coming out because your life matters to you, and this other person matters to you, and you want that other person to know who you really are.

I love this book. I recommend it all the time. I hope you'll read it. What I hope most is that it will shift progressive Christian readers from a quiet position of tacit acceptance to a proud coming out of authentic hospitality that ruptures this world, trapped as it is by so many things, and discovers the virtues of queer Christianity.

FOR FURTHER READING
E. Edman, *Queer Virtue: What LGBTQIA People Know About Life and Love and How It Can Revitalize the Church*, Beacon Press, 2017.

THE HERESY OF RESPECTABILITY

Here's a question: you are a part of or at least familiar with churches that host soup kitchens, or groups of Christians who serve food through hunger ministries. Yes?

Now, let's ask: do you know churches who simply get together and then go eat at soup kitchens?

The difference between serving a free meal or gathering with all those who need a free meal in order to eat with them, is navigated according to the parameters of "respectability."

Going to leave "respectability" in scare quotes throughout this post, so that we always call it into question while still using it.

So...

... the demands of "respectability" diminish Christian witness. There is a general middle-class captivity of the church in North America that keeps the faith trapped in a prison of its own design.

The concept of "respectability" is a function of class. And since the majority of middle-class Christians rarely ponder class, it's not surprising that "respectability" is simply assumed in Christian faith communities rather than examined and critiqued. And such "respectability" is also inextricably tied up in issues of race and power.

Consider some aspects of respectability culture:

People call for "civility" when their power is challenged (especially if those challenging are people of color).

Some voices are labeled "divisive" if they challenge the norms that maintain current power imbalances.

One form of "respectability" polices language. There are things that can be said, and things that ought to remain unsaid. According to "respectable" Christianity, Christians aren't supposed to swear, and discourse in Christian community is supposed to be moderate, careful, nice.

Ask a pastor how often they are in a room in which people are swearing, and when it is made known that they are a pastor, the whole room apologizes and the language "improves."

Yet some of the most powerful Christian speech in our world emerges from artists and other leaders who refuse to conform to middle class respectability, and their art, their music, their speech is typically excluded from the category "Christian", because the demand for "respectability" in liturgy and preaching supersedes other demands like truthfulness, or justice, or beauty.

Try to imagine worship music that is truly authentic, that emerges from the voice of the people, rather than from the simulacrum of middle class-ness (which humorously auto-spellcheck wants to correct to middle crassness). It would sound like language bubbling up from the people. It would not be evaluated by committee. It would discomfit.

Some creatives are attempting such worship. Think for example of the Beyoncé Mass. But of course, a Beyoncé Mass only pushes out from middle class respectability in a couple of directions. But once you realize that middle class respectability is a cage with wide bars, you can step out of it in many directions.

For example, who ever made up the idea that you had to dress up for church? It's certainly not biblical. As far as we can tell, whenever Jesus worshipped, he wore the same cloak he always wore (which was probably soiled and smelly) and entered the sanctuary barefoot.

Faith communities that demand by their homogeneity a certain way of dress, a certain type of car to park in the parking lot, or whether to drive a car at all, all of these throw off certain values of "respectability."

But "respectability" extends far beyond dress code and speech patterns. It's also about the content of speech, the form of life, the values that are assumed as dominant. What kinds of topics are off limits in your community? Who is excluded when such topics are excluded?

Pay attention to "respectability," and bring it into relationship with Scripture. You see immediately how heretical "respectability" is as a replacement for the moral vision of Scripture. The Bible cares little at all about whether you live in a single-family dwelling, drive the right car, or drop scatological terms into your conversation.

Want examples of non-"respectability" in Scripture? They are legion.

Remember those Israelite spies who go into Jericho and stay with Rahab the prostitute?

Or consider Rahab's great-grandson David. Remember that story in the Bible, when Saul needed to go into a cave to take a dump, and David was hiding in the cave? He sneaks up to Saul while is indisposed, and cuts off a corner of his cloak, then presents the corner of the robe later to Saul to show that he had refused to kill him.

We could go on and tell the stories of the prophets. Ezekiel laid on his left side for 390 days. Isaiah wandered around naked. Hosea married a prostitute.

Paul the apostle boasts of beatings, imprisonments, and his general foolishness. In fact, he calls himself a fool.

And then let's not even get started with Jesus, who seems at every opportunity to undermine the "respectability" of religion, even the respectability of God. The Son of God always and consistently gravitates to the least "respectable" person, typically touching or being touched by them.

It's all reminiscent of that song in the opening of Joyce's Ulysses (a book that itself respectably undermined the "respectability" of "literature"):

I'm the queerest young fellow that ever you heard
My mother's a Jew, my father's a bird.
With Joseph the Joiner I cannot agree
So here's to disciples and Calvary.
If anyone thinks that I amn't divine
He'll get no free drinks when I'm making
    the wine
But have to drink water and wish it were plain
That I make when the wine becomes water again.
Goodbye, now, goodbye! Write down all that
    I said
And tell Tom, Dick, and Harry I rose from the
    dead.
What's bred in the bone cannot fail me to fly
And Olivet's breezy ... Goodbye, now, goodbye!

Only the freedom of non-"respectability" allows a truth-teller to play fast and loose with traditional norms, and just so step out of the prison established by the controls of "respectability." It is only beyond "respectability" that the rich find themselves proximate with the poor, addicts feel comfortable in church pews, failures preach from the pulpit, and the dirty find their way to the font.

And not to be made "respectable," mind you. No, if the heresy of "respectability" is to be undermined completely, we need to remember the waters of baptism were already dirty to begin with, that dirt is life, and God is in the muck.

FOR FURTHER READING

D. Marx, *Status Culture: How Our Desire For Social Rank Creates Taste, Identity, Art, Fashion, and Constant Change*, Viking, 2022.

22

THE YOUTH

What counts as church? In modern church life I think there has been a strong focus on programs. Programs are from the modern church viewpoint the church in action.

As an example, as a pastor who has worked in youth ministry for a long time, I've always assumed a major or even primary responsibility was the coordination of youth programs. Plan youth events. Organize a youth group. Offer Sunday school.

Such programs are typically run by staff or volunteers working at the pace of staff and are primarily for the members of the church.

However, some recent conversations with our staff, plus simple meditation on how I actually move in the world these days as a pastor, has me reconsidering what I count as youth ministry.

Here are the examples:

- I DM (Dungeon Master) a weekly D&D group with some high schoolers, most of whom are members of our church but don't attend worship frequently. This group is more regularly active than our high school "youth group."
- I started substitute teaching during the pandemic to relieve teacher shortages.
- I coach soccer.
- Our congregation organizes and hosts Queer Camp, a camp that is not primarily for our own member youth though it does include them. It's for LGBTQIA+ youth in the region who desire time and space to be with their community in a safe and affirming environment.
- We put ourselves on the line advocating for youth-related issues including food insecurity and trans youth medical care.
- Some summers more youth walk in our Pride parade float with us than attend the average youth group gathering.
- We partner frequently with social justice related youth organizations in town. We are in relationship to them and support them.
- We've launched ministries that significantly impact minority youth, including Canopy NWA (refugee resettlement), and Ozark Atolls (Marshallese

community advocacy). Both of these groups provide care resources for youth.

- Many schools and youth-focused non-profits know us and make use of our church campus for their programming, from debate teams to theater groups to rock bands.
- The number of youths who come for 9 a.m. Sunday school may be small but the number of youth we hang out with weekly is big.

Looking at this list, I observe at least some of the following characteristics:

- In our practice youth ministry is a ministry of integrated presence. We serve and play together with young people in our community purely for its own sake, because it is good to do so.
- Some of our most successful youth programming is not exclusively or even primarily for our own church members.
- As a professional pastor (I serve full-time as a pastor supported financially by the church) I devote a considerable amount of my time not necessarily to organizing church youth programs but in service to improving the lives of young people in our community.
- We're militant about not proselytizing. We affirm

the faith traditions of the groups and youth with whom we partner.

- I have a feeling the average young family with kids in our congregation is uncertain, for a variety of very good reasons, about their own commitment to participation in ongoing youth programs. But they do want their children to grow up in a congregation that cultivates the values we do.

I line all this out in an attempt to analyze the practice theologically. A historical touchpoint in Lutheran theology is the concept of vocation. Basically, Lutherans have understood the primary context for Christian ministry as taking place in daily life.

Luther chafed against the idea that certain lifestyles (for example, monasticism) might be considered more holy than others. He famously remarked that changing diapers was a holy occupation, and more holy than a monastic in their cell precisely because someone changing a diaper is unlikely to believe that what they are doing is a special, elevated religious activity.

Now, this is not exactly like the phenomenon in "Christian" America where "Christian" businesses publish directories and put Bibles out in their waiting rooms. The Lutheran sense of vocation isn't that one should or can Christianize or have a special Christian way of repairing cars.

Rather, vocation for Lutherans is simply neighbor love. You

change a diaper because the baby needs it. You repair cars and repair them well because it benefits the driver.

Perhaps this is the core problem with the idea of church programs. There is a risk of elevating them in our minds or even in practice so that we conclude that as a church activity the youth group we organize or the Sunday school classes we plan count more than, say, youth organizing for positive change in public schools because they are grounded in the ethics their faith tradition stewards.

[I would add an important historical note here: until the 18th century Sunday school didn't exist, and until the 20th century youth groups didn't exist. Both are very modern developments in church life, and the church prior to those centuries found ways to be church without those age-specific programs.]

So let me attempt a somewhat subtle analysis here: it's difficult to discern in such secular spaces how the church is supposed to think about such activities qua church. Is there any useful distinction to be made at all between a D&D group that just plays D&D and a D&D group where there is an awareness that the game master and participants are connected to a church?

This is a very difficult question to answer because of the phenomenological complexity. If the pastor who DMs the game is really doing it just to "reach" the players, then there is a useful distinction to be made in the negative sense. I'd be opposed to such a practice on Christian grounds because I don't believe relationships should be instrumentalized for proselytization.

However, in the sense that a pastor like me is called to give of their time to youth in the community, such an awareness becomes a heuristic for deciding whether to spend the time and how much can be spent. The same kind of analysis happened when I brought the idea of substitute teaching before our church council: they unanimously felt it was a good use of their pastor's time both to meet a need and because of the benefits of presence in the school.

To be honest, in 2024 our own congregation sometimes struggles to sort out how much energy we want to put into traditional youth programming like Sunday school and youth group. Some folks like it, more people say they want it than actually attend it, and the aspects of our youth programming that attract the most attendance, grant dollars, and energy are things like Queer Camp that are unique contributions to the wider community and social justice focused.

So, if I step away from my long-standing habit of organizing youth programs and ask myself instead what church in the youth space might do if it wasn't attempting to revivify such programs, I'd keep leaning into the practice of presence and integration. If we did so consistently as a whole church, I think we'd prioritize the following habits:

- We'd watch for what the youth are already doing and organizing and join them (rather than trying to organize or get them to do things with us).

- We'd invite all youth more directly into all aspects of the life of the church that are uniquely church—worship leadership, social actions, study and prayer.
- We'd consolidate youth activities so they are integrally connected to these core practices (this last one we're already doing because we're going to experiment with a developmentally appropriate "Sunday school" for the younger children that occurs during the sermon).
- We'd find more effective means of equipping parents to integrate Christian commitments into their daily life. As a whole church, this might mean making a concerted effort to be greener, to organize against government and corporate abuse of the poor, and to structure more of our family time in order to live our individual vocations well in daily life.
- Be ready, as the need arises, to innovate and launch programs like Queer Camp that meet an actual need rather than simply perpetuate what is assumed as de rigueur.

Why does this all matter? Well, it's all me trying to shift my personal attention from putting energy into things I emphasize to myself more out of habit and nostalgia than anything else, and then honor and recognize that many things we may not name as "youth programming" are precisely that, but better and more vocationally true and really just a lot of fun and impactful.

Readers might ask themselves, as I am asking myself as a pastor and dad: what do we want or desire out of youth programming? Do we even know? We make choices all the time about what our children will sign up for and commit to, from Girl Scouts to soccer to D&D clubs to marching band to summer jobs. How do we make such choices, and do our convictions inform such choices?

Our decisions around worship participation, volunteering in the church, attending church programs, and participating in the wider (and ever more demanding) set of demands of secular life currently lack balance. We know this because most of us are on some levels dissatisfied. Either we feel over-committed, or we feel frustrated that we struggle to schedule those things we actually value, or on some levels we commit ourselves to activities and we don't even know why.

The demands of our situation are insatiable, and the new media landscape overwhelms us with formational resources that overwhelm any chance that the one hour of worship on Sunday morning can compete. For example, I recently listened to an interview on The Daily with a conservative evangelical pastor driven out of his parish in Fort Smith by the rise of Trumpism. If you listen to the interview, you get the sense he'd been doing his level best to form a community, a growing community, only to discover between 2016-2020 that the majority had willingly bought into the falsehoods of Qanon.

The result: an existential crisis for the pastor. If everything he had been doing with his parish still resulted in them believing such false things, had he been doing it all wrong?

What was the value of all that time in worship and programs if it didn't buttress them against manipulative lies and fealty to a morally problematic leader?

No wonder those of us in the emerging landscape of progressive church have a certain level of skepticism about engaging our people at the intensity level of the evangelicals. We're uncertain that would be healthy or effective. But more likely there's also a kind of secular complacency, a willingness to be populated in our use of time by all the demands of modern life. That's less good and progressives more than anyone else should be skeptical of the way the systems around us wish to catechize us.

Perhaps this is the way forward, to ask ourselves what youth ministry looks like if the goal is to equip and strengthen our communities for resistance and resilience.

FOR FURTHER READING
R. Murray, *Made, Known, Loved: Developing LGBTQIA Inclusive Youth Ministry*, Fortress Press, 2021.

23

A PROGRESSIVE CHRISTIAN ACCOUNT OF CRITICAL RACE THEORY

Smart messaging has long been critical to political success. Think "Contract With America" or "Fake News." Often, these messages carry more emotional impact than anything else, tapping into the affect and worldview of those who resonate with them. Academics construct messaging also, and sometimes those terms make their way into wider academic usage. One academician who has had greater impact than many is Kimberlé Crenshaw, who coined the term "intersectionality" and also the phrase "Critical Race Theory."

What is rare: when the parlance of academia (and in this case, a term used primarily in legal circles as a more focused application of critical theory in legal studies) makes its way into the national messaging of a conservative political group. And yet, that's what you have with Critical Race Theory. You can read about it all over the place now. School board candidates are campaigning against the possibility of it influencing school curriculum. Entire Christian denominations are publishing social statements rejecting it.

The paranoia that surrounds the term is remarkable. Entire hate groups like Moms for Liberty have organized to supposedly root it out of public-school education. Most people encountering the term have no idea what it actually means. Try it out: post in social media or ask in a party, "How would you define Critical Race Theory?" See how people respond.

WHAT IS CRITICAL RACE THEORY?

In a sense, it's quite simple. Critical race theory is the application of critical social theory by scholars who want to look critically at our legal systems and race. As Nixon-appointed former Supreme Court Justice Harry Blackmun wrote: "In order to get beyond racism, we must first take account of race. There is no other way."

Critical theory argues that many problems have their roots more in societal structures and cultural assumptions than individualistic factors. CRT assumes that social ills like racial injustice can be repaired through a focus on changes in societal structures and cultural assumptions. We need to change our laws (like zoning laws that result in redlining) and our cultural assumptions (like the ones that led one woman to have her house appraised at $100,000 more when she removed signs of her ethnicity and had white friends show it to the appraiser).

It's not enough to simply say, "I don't dislike black people." Or: "My kids play with the neighbors who are African American." That has little to do with structural injustices baked into our legal system.

You can see how a political party like the Tea Party with libertarian leanings would chafe against critical theory. You can also see how many Americans, trained as they are in hyper-individualism, would doubt any analysis of race that is focused on societal structures. Many atomistic assumptions get in the way. "I worked hard to get where I am." "Why are you trying to make me feel ashamed about being white?"

What Critical Race Theory does is take account of race as it relates specifically to the law, and then asks, "What laws need changing to repair a system constructed, at least in part, on a racially unjust basis?" Intriguingly, what Critical Race Theory is not is a pedagogy for public schools. Nor is it a pedagogy schools are planning to implement. In that sense, the "smart messaging" by the Right is a kind of gaslighting. They bring Critical Race Theory up, then school boards and educators have to defend themselves against a thing that isn't a thing.

HOW CAN WE THINK THEOLOGICALLY ABOUT CRITICAL RACE THEORY?

There are a couple of surprising things about conservative Christian resistance to Critical Race Theory. The first has to do with their typical view of the relationship between Christ and culture. The typical conservative assumption is that "the world" is in a sense at odds with "the gospel." The call is to resist "worldly" things and hold to the faith, even if that is unpopular.

It's unfortunate that conservatives who resist conformity to this world can't see that such conformity includes conformity to structural racism. "Be not conformed to this world but be transformed by the renewing of your minds" (Romans 12:2) is a rather succinct description of critical theory, to be honest. Furthermore, Christian faith places central to its practice the act of repentance, followed by repair. A central aspect of repentance is recognizing the sin and naming it. To paraphrase the late Supreme Court Justice, "To get beyond sin, we first have to take account of it." All critical theory does is identify and name sin, the sin baked into systems.

Finally, and this is crucial, Christianity itself has resources for the naming of structural evil and sin. Consider Ephesians 6:12: "For our struggle is not against enemies of blood and flesh, but against the rulers, against the authorities, against the cosmic powers of this present darkness, against the spiritual forces of evil in the heavenly places." Certainly, Christians shouldn't ignore that this text is gesturing towards forces even beyond earthly and societal, actual evil spiritual beings; but obviously this text is also referring to "rulers" and "authorities," both of whom have the power to enact laws and other forces that create harm, harm far worse in many instances than our smaller, individual sins. At least one demonic force in this world is the conspiring together of cultural forces: "What I mean is there is a death pact between our political structure and our economic overlords, and they will take us all with them with little to no forethought" (Lenny Duncan).

In this sense, a theological account of Critical Race Theory would simply recognize that, in addition to the individual joy and promise and freedom that comes with experiencing God's grace in Jesus Christ, the biblical understanding of that grace also has a societal, political, cultural, systemic component. God redeems not just the individual sinner, but the legal systems that oppress. God's grace applies not simply to your spiritual poverty, but also is transforming how we relate to our legal and economic systems so that poverty is overcome.

We can call this Critical G(Race) Theory, because it recognizes grace extends more to societal structures and cultural assumptions even than to individualistic factors. God doesn't just love individual persons. God loves cities, nations, peoples. God loves creation, ecosystems, planets, solar systems. Grace applies to these as well, in its own way, because grace is the nature of God. So then of course Critical Race Theory finds resonances with Christian faith, because Christian faith is interested in anything that causes harm and opposes grace. Analysis of those things allows us to name sin. Resistance to such analysis is itself unChristian, because it is a form of denial.

WHAT ABOUT RACE ITSELF?

Is the whole focus on racism itself important for Christian faith? Some conservative Christians seems to think, along with conservatives more generally, that a focus on racial injustice is a form of racism itself, because it attends to something we should ignore. They say, "I don't see color."

We might start by saying this: "Before we immediately dismiss it, perhaps a good Christian response is to at least entertain that we may be blind to our own sin. There's that whole log in my own eye thing, after all." But more specifically, we simply can't ignore that race is addressed in Scripture itself. To name just a few examples, you have the Israelites called out as a particular nation and people. Later, in the New Testament, you have the issue of the relationship between the gospel and the extent to which it applies to the Gentiles.

Given these discussions occur in the Scripture itself, it seems very odd that Christians would resist critical approaches to the telling of the story of America. What exactly are we afraid of? Do we hate the people of God narrated in Scripture because we learn there, they were far from perfect, sometimes awful? Does this make us despise Scripture or God or Christ? Quite the opposite. A truthful accounting of our sinfulness as the people of God is crucial to Christian witness.

Why would we be afraid of telling the story of the more horrible sides of U.S. history? Is the United States more perfect somehow? Does it need its narrative white-washed to maintain national identity? A national narrative that requires propaganda in place of the truth is nationalism, not patriotism. Real patriots find it intrinsic to their patriotism to critique their nation. Faithful Christians, and proud citizens of any nation, have nothing to fear from critical theory and a racial analysis of injustice. Quite the opposite, we know and trust that God's grace shows up and redeems precisely in and through such critique.

FOR FURTHER READING

K. Crenshaw, *Critical Race Theory: The Key Writings That Formed the Movement*, The New Press, 1996.

PART V

POLIS

CLIMATE CHANGE

The church in its social-historical aspect is always already functioning as an important political actor. This means that it exists and acts politically, before it explicitly takes up any particular political position, and before any questions are raised about the criteria for its current political stance. The usual presumption of an a priori 'neutrality' and 'political innocence' is either uncritical, or or deliberately veils existing political alliances. It is essential to develop a critical-political hermeneutics of the church in order to keep the church from identifying itself uncritically and without any checks with particular political ideologies (*Faith In History and Society: Toward a Practical Fundamental Theology*, Johann Baptist Metz, 88).

L et's accept Metz's assertion as a profound truth. The church is always already functioning as an important political actor. This will come as a shock to many ears, because many if not most contemporary American Christians rather uncritically assume that the so-called doctrine of separation of church and state means that the church can exist in a kind of neutral religious space, "politically innocent" as it were.

Before the church takes up any political position, it is already functioning as a political actor. Perhaps this can help shed some light on the experience we are having in supposedly more polarized political contexts. There, the political polarization as it impacts church life is exposing/unveiling the church as an inherently political actor.

Of course, this may be because many churches or even the church in general has uncritically identified with political ideologies. But it's important for us to make this distinction: it's not that the church shouldn't be political—it always already is —but rather that the work of the church is to be political in the right way, with an awareness that it is in fact a priori political.

The year after the end of the hottest summer on record, we might ask ourselves what it has meant for climate change that the church has, especially in the U.S. context presumed itself neutral and politically innocent.

To what extent has the church aided and abetted climate change?

As a moral voice the church has been very late to the game in the climate crisis. Much if not most of impactful climate activism has arisen out of secular spaces. Although some resources have emerged in the last decade (like the *New Creation Liturgies*) centering creation care from a Christian perspective, for the most part those who have been our prophets for climate change have understood the church to be complicit in climate change rather than a vital partner in solidarity with climate activism.

The complicity is theological. The church has for the most part read Scripture with an anthropological lens, concerned primarily with the salvation of humans and much less with our relationship with creation as a whole. In spite of a rather deep leitmotif in Scripture of God's abiding relationship with all of creation and humans as woven into it, the church has prioritized a gospel focused on saving human souls for a future or separate heaven.

All kinds of brutal systems have arisen from this theological error. Creation has been understood, in the worst cases, as a disposable vessel, as something humans can lord themselves over, or in the most common cases, simply as not a significant part of whatever it is that Christian faith is to be concerning itself with.

Christian theology in many quarters has for the most part simply been silent in relationship to creation, and just so inadequately prepared to address the climate crisis.

So, what should we do?

In all instances, I believe the first move is the hardest to wrap our heads around but also the most essential. We truly must disabuse ourselves of the false notion that the church is apolitical. We must overcome the concept, so commonly taught among us, that we might somehow, in separating church from an influence over the state or the state having influence to keep us from being church in certain ways, arrive at some spiritual state of political innocence in which spiritual or religious life is not political.

In other words, we must realize that church properly understood is an alternative politics.

Once we wake up and remove the veil, then we can begin to understand everything in Scripture and Christian tradition that sees church as an "outpost of the kingdom of God" in the way it should be seen, as itself a kind of politics. As a kind of politics, it has something (quite a lot in fact) to say about our relationship to our industrial and economic practices that are contributing to climate change and that sacrifice (especially) the poor and workers at the altar of a neoliberal economy.

My parishioner Terry Tremwel, retired professor of sustainability at the University of Arkansas and a vocal advocate for solar and other green solutions to the climate crisis, regularly points out that the climate crisis exacerbates essentially all other social injustices we concern ourselves with as a church. Whether it's refugee resettlement, poverty, or anti-racism work, each of these cultural issues will be dramatically impacted by climate change because the effects of climate change play out primarily in geographical contexts where the poor and oppressed live. The rich, on the other hand, will be able to either move to places more secure from climate catastrophe, or construct built environments that mitigate the impacts.

In this, he agrees with renowned theologian Catherine Keller:

> It is so-called civilization that has brought us to this moment of self-contradiction, at which point we are too busy responding politically to immediate threats to vulnerable human populations—of black lives, of immigrant, uninsured, or sexually abused lives—to mind the matter of the earth.

Often climate justice and other social justices are intimately entwined. Some of the solutions to economic inequality in the United States could address climate change. For example, canceling student debt (which would increase Black wealth by 40%) could have as a byproduct greater investment in green energy solutions. University graduates, freed up from college debt, might choose to incur new debt invested in solar solutions or electric cars.

Similarly, a universal basic income might have a broad impact. Imagine everyone at every income level suddenly receiving enough income to afford an electric bicycle or even payments on an electric car or the installation of a heat pump as their source of heating and cooling.

Or perhaps most crucially, imagine campaign finance reform that restructures politicians' self-interest. Freed up from the influence of wealthy corporate donors, their voting might more consistently comport itself with the actual self-interests of voters and the necessities of life together on this planet.

Underneath all these economic concerns is an even more

crucial issue, that of climate change. And if we look at the climate crisis, we can see that in many ways the deleterious effects of human economy on the climate come not from the failures of our current economic system, but precisely from its successes. Our economy has flourished (for some more than others) through our voracious consumption of fossil fuels and the growth of the human population on the planet. Scientists now label this geological era the Anthropocene because of how extensive human impact is on Earth's geology and ecosystems as a whole, in particular anthropogenic climate change.

We have before us a triple threat: 1) the left and the right are caught up in a culture war that 2) largely distracts us from the more significant issue of economic injustice, and 3) underlying all of this is climate change, a more cataclysmic issue that requires even larger and significant interventions than either cultural problems or economic injustice.

Considering this, what are progressive communities of faith called to do? Of course, at a macro-level, slowing the dramatic climate change we are now seeing must be accomplished at the level of federal regulations and corporate policies. Each of our individual choices to recycle our milk bottles is, though important, a drop in the bucket compared to the massive CO_2 output of transportation, followed closely by electricity and industry. They may even be practices of denial.

If you want to personally cut down on greenhouse gas emissions, stop flying in an airplane. One return flight from London to Rome, for example, produces more greenhouse gases than the amount produced by citizens of 17 countries annually.

But unless market pressures truly push solar and other sources of energy to the point where they are less expensive per kilowatt than fossil fuels, industries will continue to govern themselves according to the market and the bottom line. Only federal and international regulations can keep corporations from focusing primarily on their bottom line.

This means the average churchgoer, or the average congregation, can move the needle on climate change more through effective political and corporate advocacy than any other method. Recycling is good, but in many ways recycling is like the distraction of the culture wars; it makes us feel like we are doing something while we actually ignore the deeper root injustices in the system. It's a form of denial.

I ask again, what can faith communities do? Well, I think we are called to model that which we want our corporations and governments to do. If we want to call on corporations to aim toward zero greenhouse gas (GHG) carbon emissions, we need to already be committed to it in our own house. It's easier to advocate for change when you are speaking out of a space of integrity.

Imagine a movement of churches going net zero GHG carbon emissions by 2030. Such communities would make two commitments. First, they conduct an energy audit to evaluate their current ecological footprint. Then, at the highest level of their organization, they commit to getting to zero carbon by 2030. Climate sanctuaries could then also advocate for zero carbon by 2030 with their denominations and hierarchies and their members, and where possible disconnect lines to natural gas and other companies who are not net zero. They also participate in state, federal, and corporate advocacy for zero carbon by 2030.

Remember Gandhi's mantra, "Be the change you wish to see in the world." Or keep in mind that leaders with integrity lead by example. Churches cannot with integrity call for zero carbon emissions when they themselves are still quite complicit. And on the flip side, if thousands of local congregations host intentional conversations and adopt as congregational policy the goal of zero carbon emissions by 2030, this will have a far broader impact than just the emissions of their local house of worship. It will influence, by example, members of congregations who work in corporations, are elected to state and federal offices, who own homes and drive cars. More than anything, it will illustrate through direct action the church is overcoming its long-standing denial.

FOR FURTHER READING

T. DeLay, *Future of Denial: The Ideologies of Climate Change,* Verso Press, 2024.

25

CAN GOD SPEAK?

Recently a couple members caught me at the office door with questions/comments. I've come to love this aspect of preaching, the way it sometimes (more or less from week to week) has legs in conversation and congregational action. In fact, I try to operate with the working theory that the sermon is far more than just the words spoken by the preacher in worship, but is literally the continuing engagement with the sermon that happens among the gathered community as the week proceeds.

This week, I had just finished up preaching on the so-called "delay of the Parousia." I'd invited the congregation to consider what it means for us in our Advent observances that we talk about Christ, invoke Christ by name in ancient texts and liturgical action, in this sense practicing his presence, always while also acknowledging his absence (which is what it means to confess that he will "come again").

It's an unusual eschatological move, a paradox, that on the one hand maintains a kind of ambiguity about why we even refer to Jesus in community at all if he isn't around, while at the same time allowing the continuing anticipation of his return to "trouble" us.

In this conversation we ended up talking about the alternatives some Christians have posited for how Christ continues to be with us. In the gospel of John it's with Christ's promised Spirit. That is how Christ stays "present."

In Matthew, it seems to be "in the least of these," which refers to Jesus' final teaching in Matthew 25 before his crucifixion: 'Truly I tell you, whatever you did for one of the least of these brothers and sisters of mine, you did for me.'

As we talked, I ended up mentioning one of the philosophical essays that has had the most enduring impact on my thinking, "Can the Subaltern Speak?" by Gayatri Chakrovarty Spivak, and lo and behold, they (my parishioner) went home and read that essay! Spivak is by no means an easy read, its poststructuralist, and I can't say I fully follow all the arguments in it. It's obscurely generative. But my member sent screenshots of passages they found particularly impactful, and then wrote,

I think I get where they are going, that we hear "God" speak basically through the voice of "the people" but if the voice of the people is oppressed then can God speak... is that what this means? And that basically we've only heard the voice of white people. Predominantly white men? Who had to suspend their own conscience when writing? Am I understanding correctly?

Although the "God" references aren't an aspect of Spivak's essay, I love how my parishioner so succinctly connects the main thesis of the essay to the topic we'd been discussing. The only thing I added was: "And also that in the same way a lot gets in the way of us hearing the subaltern speak, a lot gets in the way of us hearing God speak. Then, since God is or identifies with the subaltern, we can also ask, "Can God speak?" and then the two topics, the subaltern being able to speak and God being able to speak become... the same question."

I find this to be an incredibly compelling way of framing how progressive Christians in particular talk about God. There is, in some ways, a reluctance to speak of God, a desire to avoid overtly religious speech. Instead, there is studied and careful focus in progressive church on language that centers neighbor-love, in particular care for, attention to the "subaltern."

However, sometimes in the same way language about God can become rote and vacuous, so too can some progressive language about justice and the neighbor. This is why essays like Spivak's raise the question they raise. *It's a legitimate and ongoing question: can the subaltern speak, speak for themselves, speak over the voices of those in power who wish to speak on the subaltern's behalf? And intriguingly, the question is not "can the subaltern be heard" but "can the subaltern speak?"*

For a progressive Christian, the parallel theological question has comparable validity. We might even say (along the lines of thinkers like Emmanuel Levinas) that the question of whether the subaltern can speak and whether God can speak are essentially the same question (because the face of God is the face of the neighbor).

At the very least, we might recognize that the question of God speaking presents many of the same problems as the question of the subaltern speaking, and that this is true is a fundamental insight of progressive Christian thought, informed as it is by thinkers like Spivak.

So now let's jump back to the "delay of the Parousia" briefly. It's largely assumed in many academic circles that this "delay" is a fundamental hallmark of the early Christian experience. It's the dominant narrative, and it is this dominant narrative that I presented and worked with in the sermon.

However, there is some scholarship on the topic that complicates the dominant narrative ... For example, in an editorial article on the topic, the editor says some of the essayists included in the volume argue that "Jesus expected an interval, and not just one between his own time and the destruction of Jerusalem: Glasson points out that the establishment of the Eucharist by Jesus is a clear sign that he envisaged a (perhaps lengthy) interval between his death and the end, a view to which Brant Pitre, a current 'delay sceptic', has recently assented" ('The "Delay of the Parousia",' Mohr Siebeck, *Early Christianity* 9 (2018), 1–7)s.

Another author in the same collection asserts the New Testament (especially in Paul) illustrates "development rather than simply contextual variation. [The author] traces a series of shifts in Paul's letters as Paul encourages his congregations to come to terms with delay. While in contrast to Wright,

Landmesser's approach envisages delays, such delays nevertheless provoke "Ambiguierung" and "Irritation" rather than crisis. Such afflictions lead to a development in Paul's letters which culminated in a greater stress on the present experience of communion with Christ."

All of this brings us back around to the question of God's speech. Do we believe God speaks "through the Scriptures"? Through the sermon? Through the sacraments? Through the community? In the face of the neighbor? In the voice of the subaltern?

In post-structuralist perspective, we can similarly ask: Do we believe the poor can speak? That the "text" of the poor is a divine revelation? Do base communities preach? Are we attentive to the face of neighbors different from us? We might argue that we will finally hear God when we finally hear the poor. And we will know whether they have truly spoken if our lives, the world, are changed in the direction of the call to action spoken by that voice.

And does God not speak in the dialogue between pastor and parishioner as they reflect on the sermon and Spivak?

FOR FURTHER READING

Ed. By R. Morris, *Can the Subaltern Speak? Reflections on the History of an Idea*, Columbia University Press, 2010.

26

SIN AND SOLIDARITY

"It is ironic that America, with its history of injustice to the poor, especially the black man and the Indian, prides itself on being a Christian nation." (James Cone)

Ironies are ironies, after all, which makes them difficult in the explication. The irony James Cone identifies in much of Christianity results from the idea that sin is primarily about personal moral failings rather than systemic powers. In which case it's no wonder Christians who believe sin to be hyper-individualistic have trouble recognizing sin that is systemic.

Add to this the widespread recognition on all sides of the issue (this is something about which conservative and liberal and progressive Christians theoretically mostly agree) that we are often unaware of our own complicity in sin. Thus, Jesus' teaching about the speck and the log (Matthew 7:3) or Paul's line in Romans 7:35: "I do not understand my own actions."

We either misunderstand what sin is; or we are in denial of sin; or we simply just don't get it. However you look at it, it becomes particularly ironic when the very same community who believes sin is primarily personal moral failure can also at the same time think a nation could be "Christian." Ironic then that in the present moment the same people who want us to be a Christian nation are vociferously combatting work like critical race theory that attempts to name national sin.

Perhaps one of the greatest dangers of progressive Christianity is a tendency toward performative gestures at justice rather than sacrificial commitment to justice itself. Progressives may be, on average, more willing to recognize than liberals the extent to which we remain complicit in sinful systems—but this is a far cry from knowing what to do, or acting on what we actually know we should do.

I certainly know this to be true about myself. I'm willing to take risks... to a point. I'm willing to sacrifice... within reason. In other words, my awareness of the extent to which I fall short of my own commitment to justice, and certainly the Christian commitment to social justice, is present, but my will to change often falters.

I think perhaps this is what some conservative Christians fail to understand about progressive Christians. When we acknowledge and name our complicity in racism, or economic injustice, etc., it's not that we hate being white and want all white people to hate themselves. It's that we believe confessing our complicity to racism is a first step toward healing and justice.

And... we don't always then immediately model resolutely the repair we see is needed. So partially we cause our own problems.

James Cone, perhaps the greatest North American theologian to emerge out of Arkansas (where I live), adds an additional layer to this topic when he calls out white theologians in his books. In *The Cross and the Lynching Tree*, for example, he points out that although prominent white theologians in the 20th century had lynching right there in front of them happening constantly, they rarely if ever connected lynching to their cruciform theologies, even though most of them connected the cross to many other forms of abuse and predicated quite a lot of their theology on an analysis of the cross of Christ.

"The conspicuous absence of the lynching tree in American theological discourse and preaching is profoundly revealing, especially since the crucifixion was clearly a first-century lynching." (*The Cross and the Lynching Tree*)

Cone argued, at least in part, this was because white theologians' theology was so inextricably tied into racial injustice that those theologians simply didn't even know what they didn't know. Or they did know and intentionally looked away. How could it be otherwise?

Unfortunately, during the course of 2,000 years of Christian history, this symbol of salvation has been detached from any reference to the ongoing suffering and oppression of human beings—those whom Ignacio Ellacuría, the Salvadoran martyr, called "the crucified peoples of history." The cross has been transformed into a harmless, non-offensive ornament that Christians wear around their necks. Rather than reminding us of the "cost of discipleship," it has become a form of "cheap grace," an easy way to salvation that doesn't force us to confront the power of Christ's message and mission. Until we can see the cross and the lynching tree together, until we can identify Christ with a "recrucified" black body hanging from a lynching tree, there can be no genuine understanding of Christian identity in America, and no deliverance from the brutal legacy of slavery and white supremacy (xiv.).

We can appreciate Elizabeth Palmer's acknowledgment in an article on James Cone in *The Christian Century*, when she said James Cone's theology is "easy to like and hard to live." Indeed. And in a sense, this is true of much of the liberation theology that informs our church practice.

As a progressive pastor I'm committed to a critical evaluation of my own theology, my own practice, all considering liberation theology, because I believe self-scrutiny is essential to the walk of faith. This is what I believe repentance to be, or at least how it starts, and I believe repentance to be at the heart of the Christian life.

And I do not think this is hating myself, or my whiteness, or my maleness. It's simply being responsible. Recognition of sin is a crucial step in the Christian journey.

What does this mean for a guidebook to progressive church, written as it is by a straight white male? Well, I've thought about that for a long time. I have some reservations about the idea that I might write "the" book on progressive church, but I feel more comfortable writing a guidebook. It's perhaps appropriate for my social location in relation to the intersections I'm near and aware of.

I think it's also important to name how I go about doing this work. Our congregation is itself predominately white. As is our denomination. I'm uncertain how that might change, but one thing I know for sure is that I am uninterested in making our church more diverse if by diverse it means those from other racial or ethnic communities have to travel a long way to come and meet us at "our" table. Instead, I value the model of allowing each community to be itself and us doing the hard work of moving in the direction of neighboring faith communities and ethnic groups who are open to shared mission and critical conversations for repair.

I made this point in a sermon a few weeks ago. Our Marshallese outreach coordinator had planned a lunch for our congregation, a thank you meal. I was worried (for good reason) that fewer members of our congregation would attend the lunch than we hoped. I simply pointed out in the sermon that our coordinator, by preparing the meal and serving it, was traveling a much farther distance (culturally, etc.) in order to meet us where we are than we seemed to be in traveling the direction of the Marshallese community.

Too much of the work of repair was being performed by him and his community. That's a typical problem in the progressive church dynamic.

Over the years we have been developing practices that I hope are really centered in reparations. These include: 1) we partner with the neighboring Marshallese community and join their voice seeking reparations for our nuclear tests on their atolls, and 2) we have been especially open as a community to providing reparative space for the queer community. 3) We're working on figuring out how as a congregation we can move past a simple land acknowledgment and toward actual reparative work related to the Osage, Caddo and Quapaw Nations, on whose ancestral land our church building is situated.

We do none of these things perfectly, and I'm not even entirely sure that we ever can. There's quite a bit of intersectional self-reflection yet to do. Perhaps especially we could open even more conversations with the communities most affected by social injustice and listen as they reflect back to us how we might live more fully into the justice of God; but we'd need to do that in ways that don't simply make those impacted communities do even more free work for us.

In the meantime, it's especially hard to navigate when the very tools we have been discovering are helpful for such work, tools we share in the public square, are under attack by the very

Christian communities who should recognize with us that the starting point for Christian "work" is repentance.

All I know to do is to keep doing my own work, and our congregational work, and try, as difficult as it sometimes is, to listen non-anxiously and grow and change. Real solidarity is not simply using others for the sake of growth, though. Real solidarity will simply mean becoming those with whom we are in solidarity, which of course is the most radical point of Cone's theology.

FOR FURTHER READING

J. Cone, *The Cross and the Lynching Tree*, Orbis Books, 2013.

27

PUBLIC CHURCH

T he public is a new sacred space for the church's ministry of justice and peace. —Ilsup Ahn

The rise of the concept of "Public Church" comes out of a progressive Christian response to Christian nationalism. Conversations about public theology, and specifically naming it "public" theology, emerge as a counterpoint to the assumption made in many parts of conservative Christianity that the state/country/nation simply is Christian, founded implicitly or explicitly on Christian values.

By contrast progressive theologians usually recognize the emergence of secular life has created a space for the free exercise of religion, or the exercise of none at all, and adaptively functions as a theology that engages a wider community of people, not all of whom are Christian and many of whom speak from no specific theological perspective at all, but nevertheless may welcome a theological contribution and voice in the public square.

Thus the practice of public church, and thinking about the voice of the church in the public, is inherently a progressive counterpoint to the subsumption of the political by the theological that happens in evangelical thought which simply assumes there is no other approach to politics than a religious one.

In the 20th century, when the American church mostly (although never exclusively) understood itself to be an entity somewhat separate from politics could, under the auspices of a concept of separation of church and state and a non partisan approach to political life, attempt to hold together people who held wildly disparate political beliefs but still understood themselves to be part of the same church. This was still in an era when belief and fidelity to specific beliefs was top of the line.

In the local church, you might be Lutheran first and then only secondarily Republican or Democrat or Libertarian and in the church, people could be committed to those political perspectives without the church splintering ecclesiologically. Forces emerged in the late 20th century making this increasingly impossible. It's probably especially centered in the work of the Moral Majority and other Christian nationalist organizations that very slowly but surely seized power in the Republican Party —so much so that today you simply can't really find Republicans who aren't also Christian (and also mostly nationalist).

In the meantime the Democrats, the only other viably large political party in American life, though still populated by many

Christians is at least theoretically, is as a matter of political ideology ecumenical and interfaith. With the slow but steady decline of church participation in the 20th century and the accelerated decline of disaffiliation in the 21st century, Republicans have been able to maintain their ties to Christianity and haven't needed a theological discourse to think about religious matters in relationship to politics; but increasingly, the left has needed such a discourse, and what has emerged is a pretty vibrant movement that we can call public theology.

It's rather fascinating that just in the last few years a number of organizations have emerged. Offices within larger university structures, naming public theology and church explicitly. Yale University now has the Center for Public Theology and Policy founded by William Barber II. The Lutheran School of Theology now has a public church track and another Lutheran seminary, United, has established a new program in Public Theology and Witness.

Clearly academic institutions have embraced the label, but what I want to do in what follows is explain why it is I find the notion of public theology or public church to be so central to progressive Christianity that I've included a whole chapter about it.

Basically, it has to do with the extent to which we strive to make church public facing and public engaging. Public facing has to do with basic neighborliness. I'm quite drawn to church practices that facilitate our church being a good neighbor in our local community. In this sense I love the long standing slogan many progressive Christian churches have use in urban centers,

"In the city for good." And although our church is not a downtown city church the slogan is still an invitation to think about how a church in a neighborhood can contribute to the good of the neighborhood first by example, in terms of what we do with our facility and model as practiced in the neighborhood, and also by offering the space for neighbors to use, in particular improving our grounds so that the neighborhood benefits from them.

In terms of public engagement, this has meant over a very long period of time bringing a voice to the conversation that happens in our community about public schools, municipal policies, county governance and state level politics.

Although I can't say this is universally true everywhere. It's definitely true in our community that conservative clergy make up a super majority in our region and state compared to liberal clergy, far more left leaning clergy show up and speak at county and city meetings than do conservatives. I am one of the more frequent contributors.

I suspect that behind the scenes hidden away from public microphones many conservative clergy do in fact work to influence those who are elected but they do so in privatized church spaces. By comparison, I take the risk of speaking in public on the record so that the voice of the church is on record in those spaces.

Over time, modeling this has resulted in increasing numbers of members of our church showing up and speaking on public matters in similar manner.

The difference between this way of speaking in the public

and the older evangelical model is instrumentally different: the primary reason clergy (or others) would speak outside of the church would be to reach the "outsider" with the gospel and hopefully gather them into the church. That's not the voice of the church contributing to public discourse, that is basic church proselytization.

What public church wagers is being one voice among contested voices, having to bear the scrutiny of diverse viewpoints, having to risk "sounding like" other voices in the shared public space even if the source for the positions articulated differ.

Most crucially, public theology is not trying to convert others to a specific religious perspective, but rather is trying to bring the perspective (at least for Christian public theologians) of Christ to the public square (or into what we might call the commons) and make the case that the perspective shared is not for the sake of furthering a religion, but rather contributing to and improving human flourishing.

This means a lot of different things. But one thing it means: those who speak in public spaces have to figure out how to state what they have to say in a non-parochial manner that makes sense to people who may come out of alternative religious traditions or no theological or church tradition at all.

Without going into an extensive survey of American history we've seen how this has worked in specific moments in history particularly well, chief among them the civil rights movement but also, for example, Christian abolitionist during slavery and most recently the poor people's campaign led by Reverend Dr.

William Barber. All of these moments were not examples of religious supremacists enforcing their perspectives in order to create a political religious regime, but rather voicing their perspective, shaped as it is by theological considerations, for the public good of all (establishing civil rights, ending slavery).

Returning to the concept of public "church" rather than public theology, the church an an organization sits in a unique third space: it is in a sense neither a religious nor a political movement. Rather, the church is a public movement that transcends both private organization (even if that is largely how churches have thought of themselves before the proposal for "public" church) and government authority by building and extending deep relationships based on justice.

The future of the progressive Christian church lies in knowing how to visibly and unabashedly be present and lead within the community and public. The church, as public church, has a responsibility to overcome its habits of neutrality and general complacency to structural injustice, and instead recommit to its role providing compassionate care for the 'least of these,' and emulating the early Christians' presence and active participation in the public space, adopting a new theological and political paradigm, in place of separation of church and state, instead the church vs. structural injustice.

FOR FURTHER READING

I. Ahn. *The Church in the Public: A Politics of Engagement for a Cruel and Indifferent Age*, Fortress Press, 2022.

WHY I AM (TRYING) NOT (TO BE)
A LIBERAL

"Liberal" is one of those squishy words that can mean many things. Originally it was a political position that advocated free markets, limited government, individual autonomy, etc. Until the mid-2010s I guess we would have called that "Conservative." Then there was the whole movement of neoliberalism, which came to its zenith-moment under Reagan and Thatcher and the world has never been the same since.

There's also a popular use of liberal that has a more cultural sense, with an emphasis on openness to emerging norms around gender and sexuality and diversity, etc.

In Christianity, the word "liberal" has an entirely other sense. In a way this sense resonates with the cultural liberalism above, because most cultural liberalism arises out of the same intellectual sense, but this "liberal" Christianity prioritizes reason and experience over doctrine—it's comfortable, for example, allowing the insights of evolution to modify or even replace assumptions about the account of creation in Genesis, without therefore evacuating the Christian faith altogether.

Liberal Christianity also more willingly embraces the modern tools of biblical interpretation, like the historical-critical method that arose in the 19th century. A liberal theologian is one who can embrace the idea that, for example, the Great Commission at the end of the gospel of Matthew was tacked on by later redactors and in all likelihood was never spoken by Jesus. Liberal theology was about the unique (and to my mind salutary) task of trying to create a "third way" beyond orthodox positivism and secular doubt.

Progressivism benefits from and operate within the orbit of liberal theology. It also shares quite a bit with the liberal cultural sensibility, and although it has serious problems with neoliberalism and classic liberalism, overall progressive movements find them to be such vast and influential economic and political regimes as to be almost impossible to resist. At best progressivism creates sites of friction, and at worst simply caves and participates in the hegemony of neoliberalism.

All of that being said, if you ask a progressive about their politics, they may tell you they're a socialist, and if you ask them about their theology, although they may point at liberation theology as adjacent, they'll be reluctant to subscribe to what is sometimes called "liberal" theology.

Now let me try to tell you why. First, the critique of liberal theology by Karl Barth and others is convincing. As profound as Friedrich Schleiermacher was (and there really can't be any question of his influence as the "father" of liberal theology) nevertheless Barth (and perhaps even more importantly Bonhoeffer) helped us see the issues with the kind of liberal theology that emerged under the influence of Schleiermacher.

The proof is in the pudding, you might say, and the reality we face is that liberal theology did in fact make itself quite comfortable with Nazi ideology. Any theology so willing to evacuate itself and move away from Christ clearly has problems. We could offer a similar analysis of any theological movements in our era that make themselves comfortable or compatible with fascism and "Christian" nationalism.

Where progressivism parts ways with liberal theology is that with Bonhoeffer (and later Dorothee Soelle and others in his tradition) it holds to Christ as the center (if admittedly with Jesus as exemplar as a primary mode). This is one reason I try *not* to be a liberal—sometimes it runs so hard in the direction of reason and experience it de-centers Christ, something I'm unwilling to do, on progressive (rather than traditionalist) grounds.

But let's go on. If that's the case, what precisely is it about "liberals," broadly construed, with which I take issue? I think Saul Alinsky states the matter succinctly: "A liberal is someone who leaves the room when an argument is about to turn into a fight."

I can state the matter like this in relationship to liberal

church life: liberals will try to keep everyone together *at all costs.* In other words, if something is divisive, even if it is right, they will choose avoidance of division in order to prioritize keeping everyone together. We see this repeated time after time in liberal churches: they want to keep the members who are LGBTQIA+ inclusive AND the members who are bigots all together in one church.

Liberals want to find common ground. God bless them, they actually believe in that idea. Liberals will try to reach across the aisle, even when those across the aisle clearly have traps in place so that when the reach occurs, there will be a violent tug.

By contrast, I understand progressives to be those who have simply come to the conclusion there is no good in compromise, no value in seeking common ground, because to seek those things is to sacrifice communities at the altar of division-avoidance.

I can still remember a conversation with a parishioner during our church split over my officiating same-gender weddings when they were legalized in Arkansas. He told me it was uncomfortable golfing Saturday mornings with his buddies because they would ask him why he attended "the gay church." He wanted to try and play golf with them without any friction while also participating in a church he believed (in the abstract) could be inclusive—just not too quickly or overtly. I was reminded of how I think about the real work of being progressive when I read a recent article in *Lapham Quarterly*. The author writes:

I went to an activist priest and asked, not unlike the lawyer in the Gospels, how a person went about "getting involved" in the struggle to bring about the kingdom of God. The priest had marched on Washington with Dr. King and I figured he ought to know. My question seemed to annoy him.

"It doesn't work like that," he told me. "You don't 'try to engage.' You give yourself to a community, you love the people, and your politics grow out of that love." Writing on the love enjoined in the New Testament, Torres says, "For this love to be true it must seek to be efficacious." (https://www.lapham squarterly.org/revolutions/no-smoke-camilo)

As a progressive, there are specific communities I have grown to love. For me it has particularly become refugees, LGBTQIA+ people, immigrants. As I have grown to love them, my politics grows out of that love. The reason I say that I am "trying" to "not be" a liberal is because it's actually not easy, it's constantly a struggle, but I want the politics that grows out of that love to be efficacious.

One thing I know is that if I love the ideal of the middle, of common ground, of arguments that never become a fight, then I end up loving that imaginary middle more than I love the communities I am actively giving myself to... I end up loving my bigoted golf buddies more than my LGBTQIA family in Christ. I think what a progressive gets that a liberal doesn't is something basic like, "You have to choose. Not choosing is a choice." There's this guy Jesus who talked a lot about that. And who was quite comfortable with being divisive. Because of who he loved.

And we know this one Jesus in a non-foundationalist manner, not as the funamentalists do who see Jesus as an overlord, but freely as a neighbor and friend, which is what maintains the appropriate difference in similarity between progressivism and liberalism.

Christian communities seldom entertain the Barthian option (can I claim Barth as a progressive?), that a radical over-against-ness in the political life of the church can arise, in fact must arise, out of the progressive church's loyalty to Jesus Christ. In short, we have neither a recoverable historical Jesus to guide us, nor a natural theology to discern, nor an inerrant and divine text to utilize as a playbook, but instead a God who maintains a relationship with us, and establishes a church, through the revelation that God is not us. The church thus established is in this very way political, a church of reconciliation, nonconformity, and of the cross.

It's okay to be different. Even more important, it's profoundly worthwhile to spend long intentional time among communities perceived to be different from the dominant cultures. Returning to the Saul Alinsky point above, there are times when those of the dominant culture will be made uncomfortable by their time spent in non-normative cultures. It's less that a fight might break out (Alinsky's point about liberals wanting to avoid fights) and more a fight-or-flight response to being made to feel awkward. Liberals do not like the loss of control they feel in such spaces. The hallmark of progressivism is the commitment to leaning into such loss, an intentional openness to being made vulnerable precisely for the sake of solidarity with those who are different. This is the prophetic move of progressives, willing difference and proximity to difference for the sake of solidarity and neighbor love.

FOR FURTHER READING

J. Jenkins, *American Prophets: The Religious Roots of Progressive Politics*, HarperCollins, 2020.

THE CHURCH IS A BUILDING

A new national study of religious worship attendance in America based on cell phone data supports a rather paradoxical conclusion: no one goes to church, but everyone goes to church.

Here's the geodata from smartphones:

Everyone goes to church: 73% of people step into a religious place of worship at least once during the year on a primary day of worship

No one goes to church: Only 5% attend services weekly, and "weekly" for the purposes of the study is defined as a very generous 36 times or more in a year (even though self-reporting numbers have always been closer to 22%)

Also: On any given Sunday around 45 million are in a place of worship (the U.S. population is 330 million)

Also: A larger percentage (21%), but still less than self-reporting (22% of Americans report they attend weekly), attend monthly

Also: Easter and Christmas are 50% higher than other Sundays

The most fascinating data point of all:

If you broaden the set to any visit at any time to a place of worship, 100% of the cell phones stop at a place of worship each year

Everybody actually does go to church. Literally.

At our church, we've started saying somewhat recently we are a community center with a chapel. Hundreds of people come through the church on a weekly basis, and only some of them are there for the "primary day of worship." Some are here for warrant clinics. Others stop to get food from the Friendly Fridge or Little Free Pantry. Others drop off and pick up their children for elementary school. Others live here. Others come to cook meals to deliver to communities at parks in town.

A popular bible camp song goes,

> *The church is not a building*
> *where people go to pray;*
> *it's not made out of sticks and stones,*
> *it's not made out of clay.*

The song emphasizes,

The church, it is the people
living out their lives,
called, enlightened, sanctified
for the work of Jesus Christ.

I mean, I get the point, and in fact many churches are built in such a way they probably need songs like this sung about them. They are primarily used for the "primary day of worship" and sit empty the rest of the week.

But a hyper-emphasis on church as not a building distracts from thinking creatively about built environments as crucial third places in community. We've so denigrated "church as building" we almost overlook churches altogether in urban planning and community development.

But ... 100% of Americans go to a church in any given year. Shouldn't this be a crucial data point for us as we plan church life together?

Let's start with the most obvious reasons 100% of people may go to a church building on any given year. They might park at church, check a PokeStop at church, vote at a church, visit a food pantry at church, or go to a funeral or wedding at a church. None of these are related to active church membership.

But many people who do not "belong" to a church nevertheless participate in events at church. They attend AA meetings, visit on a neighborhood board game day, eat at a summer holiday picnic, organize with the local Food Not Bombs group, or serve through a ministry of the church.

Not all churches are going to be particularly well-situated to embrace the breadth of these uses. If churches hyper-prioritize worship as the main purpose for the building, and if the primary focus of their mission is proselytization and a drive toward worship attendance, then the hyper-focus of their design will be on those uses for a building.

Progressive churches may be particularly well-suited to approach designing the physical spaces they inhabit to encourage neighborly love, healing, etc. Good Shepherd Lutheran Church (the congregation I have now served for thirteen years as pastor) has, according to one young member, "been designed with a high level of intentionality and you can feel it."

I think that's right. But you can also observe how church mission focus has shifted over the years and approaches to design have changed. The church started as a small sanctuary, then in later years expanded with a larger sanctuary. Finally, about twenty years ago a special center was added to the building, a multi-purpose room the size of a basketball court, plus a stage, multiple classrooms, and a kitchen.

In these stages of the development of the church, it was clear the church believed the building was first for worship, and then with the addition of the center, a space for education and congregational activities.

More recently, we have slowly been adding design elements that focus more outwardly, serving the neighborhood. These include the Little Free Pantry (the LFP movement started at GSLC and has now spread to every continent on the planet), an outdoor labyrinth accessible to the neighborhood, a columbarium (where ashes of those who have died can be committed and a public space for prayer and worship), a Friendly Fridge, enough solar panels to provide all our electrical needs, and now most recently a shower facility.

Next on the agenda is converting more of our space to provide shelter for LGBTQIA+ experiencing houselessness, and if we can, upgrading one of our kitchens to a commercial level so it can be used as a teaching kitchen and for more easily prepared community meals.

Even those portions of the church that had been centered around worship are now shifting toward community center use. We rent the center out to a neighboring Marshallese church who had lost their lease, have converted some classrooms into the Rainbow Closet (a gender-affirming clothing exchange), use our space to host community focused camps, and have started a whole additional ministry, Ozark Atolls, that provides community resources for the Marshallese community.

Meanwhile, all around our church the city is changing. Our city opened a food recycling station in our church parking lot and right next to it installed a large flood mitigation ditch to address water management issues nearby. On the other side of the church new housing is going up. We are serving in a neighborhood where all the conversations about "New Urbanism" hit the ground and apply.

But returning to the data with which we started, that 100% of Americans visit a church each year. Here's what has begun to intrigue me in the conversation on New Urbanism...

Churches don't show up.

Like, if you read a book about new urbanism, it doesn't include churches. If you look at maps and plans, they don't assume churches. It's literally as if in the new urbanism, churches aren't part of the built environment.

But why?

Well, we should first note many approaches to new urbanism are aligned with the values of Christianity. For example, it's no accident that our congregation AND our city both built sustainable solar power installations in approximately the same period.

In fact, local churches should likely champion many of the impulses of new urbanism, from walkability to sustainability to the commitment to community and neighborliness.

But I'm asking about the buildings themselves.

You know. Church buildings.

Where should they appear in the new urbanism? Or how should they be rehabilitated or made new?

I can only conclude that churches are absent from the built environment imagined by new urbanists either because a) new urbanists are largely agnostic, or b) the church has made itself mostly irrelevant to local neighborhoods.

For the time-being, I'm going to drop "a)" and let new urbanists answer this question for themselves. I don't know how many of them are agnostic. Maybe their religiosity goes so deep that the faith is embedded in the new urbanism itself and churches become superfluous (in which case I'd invite them to look at our church building and how it is used as counterargument against sublimating churches).

But I can speak to "b)" and there, the answer is resoundingly YES. Churches have made themselves mostly irrelevant to local neighborhoods. I've discovered repeatedly over the course of my career as a pastor that people in the neighborhood have no idea what the churches right next door to them are up to, or who goes there.

For churches to impact new urbanism, they will need to do at least three things.

- Become actively involved in the planning of their own neighborhood. When proposals for bike lanes are reviewed, or the city commission makes long range plans for intentional growth, wise churches will be present, articulate, and helpful. As the church.

- Think of their church building as integral to the built environment of their city, and remodel accordingly. Maybe this means redesigning the parking lot to better manage wastewater. Or maybe it means turning a portion of the grounds into a park with a labyrinth that encourages meditation. Or re-design the public spaces on the church property to meet emerging needs—construction of tiny homes would be a recent example. It might even mean that the church members intentionally live within walking distance of the church, and then walk to church, much like Sabbath-observing Jewish communities (and to make this work many

churches would have to address housing
affordability issues in their own neighborhoods).

- Push for policies and plans in their city that
  contribute not just to the good of new urbanism,
  but to justice in the city. Let's be honest, a lot of
  new urbanisms are class confined. So, churches will
  play a crucial role in encouraging the development
  of truly affordable housing, as well as the
  development of resources for the homeless and
  marginally housed.

Churches can add to the conversation by creatively
proposing church as "public space" or exploring how it is
important third space, spiritual space.

So too, we can consider additional issues of justice that the
church will likely center more frequently than new urbanists,
influenced as they are by moneyed and political interests.

For church buildings to recover their place at the center of
neighborhoods and urban environments, there will have to be a
conscious effort born from an awareness of the cultural crisis in
our country. The Congress for the New Urbanists (CNU) is a
non-partisan and non-sectarian organization that can support
any community, including religious communities, interested in
urbanism. New Urbanists, Bess asserts, need to avoid becoming
a tool of the real estate industry and make themselves available
to cultural and religious institutions. Historically, religious
communities have been patrons of good architecture and

urbanism. More recently, the New Urbanists have already worked on projects that have overcome the problems of zoning ordinances, street design, and parking regulation by obtaining a designation of an area as a Traditional Neighborhood District (TND), which overrides the established legal structure. These projects necessarily involve public processes in which local church communities could certainly take part (from *Building Jerusalem* by Kathleen Curran Sweeney).

Finally, let's return to that other data point and reality: no one goes to church.

The number of people in our culture who now attend church weekly, the committed core, is about 5% of the population. That's not huge.

Or is it? Because a lot of social change scholars now say you only need 3 percent for critical mass, sometimes called the "3 percent rule." A critical mass of just 3 percent of the population is required to generate major change in many situations, is another important element in successful change. Successful social movements throughout history, like the civil rights movement and the LGBTQ rights movement, have adhered to this norm.

According to J. Bruce Stewart's 3 percent rule, a small but devoted group of people can bring about change through deliberate, long-term effort. This can include organizing protests, gathering supporters, and getting their message out through social media and other channels.

The American fight for civil rights is a great example of how the 3 percent rule works. Martin Luther King Jr. and a small core of other committed activists served as the movement's leaders. They were able to get more people to support them because they planned their actions and used persuasive language.

Then, once you have the 3%, the next benchmark is the 25% tipping point, when a quarter of a group agrees with a certain point of view or acts in a certain way, it can become the new norm.

Well, that's not far off from how many Americans attend church monthly.

Finally, the rule of 150. The Dunbar rule. You can only know 150 people well. Well, the church I've been describing, GSLC, isn't far off from that number in terms of active members. And we find it's a highly effective size, small enough to be nimble, large enough to have impact.

I guess that's a lot of statistical analysis just to show how a normal little church even in the era of decline, when no one goes to church anymore, can still take us all to church.

FOR FURTHER READING

T. Gorringe, *A Theology of the Built Environment: Justice, Empowerment, Redemption*, Cambridge University Press, 2002.

PART VI

PRAXIS

WHAT, TO A PROGRESSIVE, IS WORSHIP?

L et's start with statistics: a Barna study last decade (https://www.barna.com/research/survey-shows-how-liberals-and-conservatives-differ-on-matters-of-faith/) indicated conservatives attend weekly worship far more frequently than liberals (62% vs. 35%); a more recent survey by Pew indicates 50% of conservatives attend worship while only 22% of liberals do (https://www.pewresearch.org/religion/religious-landscape-study/political-ideology/); the younger generations skew liberal and also are more likely to be religiously unaffiliated; or if you look at political parties, about 79% of Republicans self-identify as Christian whereas only 55% of Democrats do (https://www.pewresearch.org/religion/2019/10/17/in-u-s-decline-of-chris tianity-continues-at-rapid-pace/).

There is undoubtedly overlap between progressive polit-ical perspective and progressive religion. So, the markers of these large sociological groups (political party, etc.) reflects accurately the general sensibilities of the smaller group (almost a Venn diagram) that is both progressive and "church-going."

We can begin with the assumption that, statistically-speaking, worship is a lower priority for progressives than other Christian groups.

That established, the interesting question becomes: Why? Answer:

- Many progressives are leery of Christian practices like worship precisely because so many conservatives worship. This is not unlike the way many Lutherans last century abandoned weekly Eucharist because it looked too Catholic, and they didn't want to appear Catholic while living as immigrants among a wider American culture that harbored anti-Catholic sentiments.
- Many other progressives are recovering from harmful experiences in the church of their youth. They are processing religious trauma and find it very difficult to even enter a church building, let alone worship.
- Other progressives are, in somewhat contemporary terminology, deconstructing, and as part of that spiritual work, are finding participation in worship complicated by their newfound skepticism around creeds, dogma, tradition.

However, there is an additional factor:

- Many progressive Christians are simply not
  convinced weekly worship is crucial to Christian
  life. They're agnostic about it.

Progressive Christianity is much more "this-worldly" than other forms of Christianity, focused on the immanent frame and action in the world. Worship, which is assumed to be primarily about the transcendent frame and other-worldly focused, is to those of this perspective simply perceived as (at best) a waste of time and (at worst) a distraction from the weightier matters of social justice and love of neighbor.

Scripture itself includes some of this kind of skepticism: the prophets were concerned that Israel's hyper-focus on "right worship" distracted from a focus on "right living." For example:

> **21** *I hate, I despise your festivals,*
>   *and I take no delight in your solemn*
>   *assemblies.*
> **22** *Even though you offer me your burnt offerings*
>   *and grain offerings,*
>   *I will not accept them,*
> *and the offerings of well-being of your fatted*
>   *animals*
>   *I will not look upon.*
> **23** *Take away from me the noise of your songs;*
>   *I will not listen to the melody of your harps.*

24 But let justice roll down like water
  and righteousness like an ever-flowing stream.
(Amos 5:21-24)

Progressivism, focused as it is on justice, will resonate with this prophetic sentiment quite strongly. You can find the same theme in the New Testament in James, where he writes, "Religion that is pure and undefiled before God, the Father, is this: to care for orphans and widows in their distress, and to keep oneself unstained by the world" (1:27).

If we think of the life of faith as movement, an ebbing and flowing, a testimony and counter-testimony, then indeed it is quite reasonable that some Christians, having witnessed the abuses of the faith and the specific complicity of Christian worship in those abuses, would distance themselves from any forms of corporate worship. But the Scriptures (to stick with them for just a bit longer) offer a counter-response to this theme, illustrated especially well in the familiar Psalm 51. In that Psalm, the Psalmists sings, *"For you have no delight in sacrifice; / if I were to give a burnt-offering, you would not be pleased."*

This sounds stark and rather final; but then that isn't the end of the Psalm. Instead, after the psalmist makes things right, through repentance and reform of life, they sing as the concluding verse of the Psalm, *"then you will delight in right sacrifices, / in burnt-offerings and whole burnt-offerings; / then bulls will be offered on your altar."*

Anyone reading this final verse of Psalm 51 is invited to fill in for "bulls on your altar" a modern replacement like "worship practices." But the point remains, Christianity includes equipment for problematizing worship, maintaining rather than abandoning it. It reminds us that worship for its own sake, or worship detached from the needs of the world, or worship that steals from the world, is unacceptable to God. It at the same time indicates that if the needs of neighbor-love and justice are met, then God can and does in fact welcome "right worship."

Worship and justice are not opposed. They are organically inter-related, with worship being "right" only when worshippers are seeking to make the world "right" first.

So now let's ask ourselves: what is worship, generally speaking? That's a big question, but we are up to the task. Worship at its most basic is praise. It's pausing long enough to say to the one worthy of worship, "You're awesome!"

Christian worship has, historically, included parts that do more than solely praise. First, worship works hard to clarify "who" is awesome. That's the whole point of creeds, a lot of our hymns, the (seemingly florid) endings and beginnings of prayers, and even the reading of Scripture in worship itself. All of these practices help the community *name* that One. *This* God but not *that* God is awesome.

Christian worship is also about *relationship* with that One, so it includes practices that create that relationship. Prayer is the primary mode for this, but so is silence. Finally, worship is a two-way relationship, so Christians anticipate in worship the

One worshipped "talks back." Christians in worship hear God speak through the texts, through the sermon, receive this God in the meal, and more generally encounter God's Spirit (affectively, etc). This is what worship is. There are other ways to talk about worship, probably lots more, but this gives us a good starting point.

Christian worship in the United States has introduced some complications here. The historic liturgies of the church, though still practiced by many denominations, gave way on the frontier to forms of worship that were quite new. Frontier worship itself had it as a kind of goal to stir up the participants into spiritual awakening to accomplish conversion. This mode of worship, the Frontier style, was then also influenced by the popularization in early America of the traveling public speaker. Think Ralph Waldo Emerson. As a result, complex church spaces that had once included multiple altars for devotion were abandoned and instead churches built "auditoriums" allowing focus on the speaker.

A church I previously served in Wisconsin illustrates this shift. The architect did something entirely unique: they put the pulpit right in the center of the altar. Churches around the country had shifted to auditorium seating, but the Lutheran architect couldn't quite bring himself to go that far, there had to be an altar, so... he cut the pulpit right into the middle of the altar. Tucked into it the preacher risks knocking over the candles or spilling the communion wine if gesticulating too wildly.

All these moves (not to mention the general move toward

"rational" worship that happened during and after the Enlightenment) resulted in a narrowing of worship, making it in many places much like a performance with an audience as much or more than an interactive experience with the holy Other.

This brings us around to "what is worship" a final time. Perhaps for the average church-goer, worship is an auditory event, a chance to "hear" things, to hear the band play, to hear a sermon. It's entirely possible the majority of those attending worship on a Sunday morning are focused (for better or worse) primarily on it as either a religious duty or an event in which they'll receive something (a helpful word).

All of this then leads back to the title question: What, to a progressive, is worship?

Let's start with a few categories we haven't yet considered for the meaning of Christian worship. **First, we might think of worship as community organizing.** Progressives believe in organizing to work for the good of ordinary people, the planet, and in particular, the poor. Since worship is still the most unique kind of event that includes every generation, every person from every walk of life, it would make a lot of sense for progressives to think of worship as the primary space in which they can organize for good.

Second, if progressives really believe that a part of leaning Left is unlearning the propaganda of the Right and continually doing the critical work necessary for

justice, then worship is a place, in fact one of the best places, to learn and grow. C.S. Lewis famously said of prayer, "I pray because I'm helpless. I pray because the need flows out of me all the time, waking and sleeping. It doesn't change God. It changes me." So too worship, even if it does nothing "for" God, is an event in and through which we all can be changed.

Worship is unique in many ways, but one way it is unique is the media it stewards, from singing to preaching to prayers arising from the people. These are practices difficult to find in almost any other context. Progressive churches can do a lot more work to ensure that the content of the hymns, the words of the prayers, the practices included in worship, are as much influenced by progressive sensibilities as anything else, but it is highly doubtful whether progressive church or progressive Christianity can benefit from dropping these practices. The point is not to cease the practices, but to change and recontextualize them.

Third (and this point cannot be emphasized enough), worship serves as an opportunity for encountering the wonderful in the everyday. Worship, precisely because it is directed toward an "Other," facilitates discovering the ordinary is revealed to be the extra-ordinary. The normal light of every day experience takes on an extra glow. It is like the Gerard Manley Hopkins poem *God's Grandeur*:

> *The world is charged with the grandeur of God.*
> *It will flame out, like shining from shook foil;*
> *It gathers to a greatness, like the ooze of oil*

Crushed. Why do men then now not reck his rod?
Generations have trod, have trod, have trod;
   And all is seared with trade; bleared, smeared
      with toil;
   And wears man's smudge and shares man's
      smell: the soil
Is bare now, nor can foot feel, being shod.

And for all this, nature is never spent;
   There lives the dearest freshness deep down
      things;
And though the last lights off the black West went
   Oh, morning, at the brown brink eastward,
      springs —
Because the Holy Ghost over the bent
   World broods with warm breast and with ah!
      bright wings.

In other words, although progressives are correct to concern themselves with the abuse of worship, the way it might be used for distraction or self-justification, they are called nevertheless to remember that worship rightly construed serves precisely some of the ends most valued by progressives.

Finally: those organizing for social justice are going to wear themselves out. Although worship may not be universally perceived as "rest"—in fact since one of the more common reasons people don't join corporate worship Sunday morning is related to exhaustion—it takes place on the day of rest for a reason. Worship is a profoundly restful practice. It's recuperative, healing, therapeutic.

A progressive who worships might think of it as a nap before the struggle, as the space in which the slogans to be chanted can be written, as the necessary pause and meet up space for those committed to alternative community.

These are idealistic and lofty goals for what progressive worship might be, but then that's progressive also: a dissatisfaction with the status quo that drives to new action.

Christian progressivism abandoning worship will never get us where we are called to go. It's part of the breathing we do as community. Maybe that's the main way to answer the original question: to the progressive, worship is a deep breath.

FOR FURTHER READING

E.D. Scott, *For All Who Hunger: Searching for Communion In A Shattered World*, Convergent Books, 2020.

DISORGANIZED RELIGION

Have you ever noticed that innovation through cooperative groups, especially larger groups, is almost non-existent? We celebrate individual innovators for a reason: innovation by cooperation or consensus is nearly impossible. Consider the idea of stigmergy from Francis Heylighen ("Stigmergy as a universal coordination mechanism I: definition and components." *Cognitive Systems Research*, vol. 38, June 2016, pp. 4-13):

> The concept of stigmergy was proposed by the French entomologist Pierre-Paul Grassé ... to describe a mechanism of coordination used by insects. The principle is that work performed by an agent leaves a trace in the environment that stimulates the performance of subsequent work—by the same or other agents. This mediation via the environment ensures that tasks

are executed in the right order, without any need for planning, control, or direct interaction between the agents.

Jesus put before them another parable:

"The kingdom of heaven is like a mustard seed that someone took and sowed in his field; it is the smallest of all the seeds, but when it has grown it is the greatest of shrubs and becomes a tree, so that the birds of the air come and make nests in its branches."

And again he said, "To what should I compare the kingdom of God? It is like yeast that a woman took and mixed in with three measures of flour until all of it was leavened."

(Matthew 13:31-34)

Heather Marsh, in an early article on stigmertic organization (accessible at: https://web.archive.org/web/20160117235400/https:/georgiebc.wordpress.com/2012/12/24/stigmergy-2/), writes: "History has shown no drastically innovative ideas that received instant mainstream acceptance and history also shows that radically new ideas are most often the result of solitary vision; to leave control of work to group consensus only is to cripple innovation."

Theologically, however, churches have typically understood themselves to be "cooperative" organizations, with each member of "the body" playing a role in contributing to the whole. The result of such "cooperative" understandings of church life has been a strange kind of paralysis and stagnation.

All you must do is read a denominational social statement (most of which have been written by committees of over a dozen people) to get a sense of what's wrong with cooperation. As Marsh also writes,

[Cooperation] is most effective only in groups of two to eight people. For groups larger than 25, cooperation is agonizingly slow, an exercise in personality management which quickly degenerates into endless discussion and soothing of ruffled feathers, is extremely vulnerable to agent provocateurs, and in large scale groups very seldom accomplishes anything of value. Cooperation traditionally operates on the democratic principle that all voices are equal, so it does not allow for leaders, or users with greater expertise, energy or understanding to have greater influence than those on the periphery. Cooperation wastes a great deal of time and resources in both discussing and discussing the discussions. In an action-based system, this discussion is rarely required as the opinion of those not doing the work is probably of little value unless it is solicited advice from a trusted knowledgeable party.

If a church of any real size places cooperation high in its values as the way it makes decisions, no wonder churches rarely step out in any specifically radical or innovative ways. The very model for moving forward is designed to stagnate, degenerate, slow, bog down. But there is another way of organizing... one we can take from our observations of the natural world. That way is... stigmergy.

Marsh continues,

> With stigmergy, an initial idea is freely given, and the project is
> driven by the idea, not by a personality or group of personali-
> ties. No individual needs permission (competitive) or
> consensus (cooperative) to propose an idea or initiate a project.
> There is no need to discuss or vote on the idea, if an idea is
> exciting or necessary it will attract interest. The interest
> attracted will be from people actively involved in the system
> and willing to put effort into carrying the project further, not
> empty votes from people with little interest or involvement.
> Since the project is supported or rejected based on contributed
> effort, not empty votes, input from people with more commit-
> ment to the idea will have greater weight. Stigmergy also puts
> individuals in control over their own work, they do not need
> group permission to tell them what system to work on or what
> part to contribute.

Now, think about your participation in the life of church.
Any church. Compare it to the cooperative model (or, perhaps
even the competitive model). How much of what you do as
church assumes cooperation as the baseline model?

How often is the operative principle, "If an idea is exciting
or necessary it will attract interest"?

How often have decisions been made by empty votes (like at
a congregational meeting)?

How often have the people with more commitment to the
idea had greater weight?

I've found it to be the case that when our church operates more in the stigmergic mode, not only does it excite or attract interest (and contributors to the work) from within the official "congregation," but also from others. Which, if you think about it, makes sense. If a track has been laid down, it's just ... there. And whoever picks up the scent of it and wants to follow ... does.

In our congregation, I can give you some examples of true stigmergic coordination. The most obvious is children helping with communion. Instead of following the cooperative model (by consensus signing up different people each Sunday to help with acolyte and communion duties) we began simply laying down a "trace." In this case the "trace" is "anyone can help, and kids seem to really like it so come help if you want." As more and more kids see it happening, more come up to help, and parents learning about it even publicize the opportunity to others via social media.

Another example: The Little Free Pantry movement, which started on our church driveway. The "trace" was an LFP itself. The community and congregation picked up the "trace" as laid down, and either take food or donate food to the pantry with no coordination, no leader, and no "consensus" vote. The first LFP was built at the whim of the founder (back to the reality that truly innovative ideas arise from a solitary vision) and did not even seek permission to construct.

I would contend that a large part of why church struggles to truly embody the kingdom of God in our world today has to do with the extent to which it has been captivated by the "cooperative" model of organization. Cooperation functions like a strange unspoken legalism that drives so much of church decision-making. Pastors often feel they can't lead apart from consensus decisions. Churches hold together disparate groups and then wonder why they can never build consensus around anything significant.

The freedom of the gospel, the freedom proclaimed by Jesus, was much more stigmergic. Jesus laid down main ideas, traces, then neither stuck around to enforce them or seek cooperation to judge them successful; and we have been trying to follow them ever since. What he didn't ever do was poll the disciples and then act only when/if he had consensus.

Imagine how different (and boring) the Jesus movement would have been if it had moved by consensus.

Imagine how different (and Jesus-like) the contemporary church would be if it moved by stigmergy.

If you have been reasonably comfortable in life, it is likely your religious practices have served as a kind of furniture to that comfort. A chair here or there may have drawn your attention to a particularly beautiful morning view, or an old couch may have discomfited your back, but nevertheless, for the most part you could rely on religion to sit down on.

Then in 2020 two events made many of us uncomfortable in ways we'd rarely experienced. There was the pandemic. And there was George Floyd. The pandemic was universal, planet-wide, and changed essentially every kind of habit we'd been in, leaving us exposed and vulnerable and searching. George Floyd's murder by a Minneapolis police officer awakened a wider set of humans across the globe to the deep injustices in our communities, particularly the injustice of police violence and systemic racism.

In the meantime African-Americans and other groups watched the majority wake a bit from their slumbers and thought to themselves, "They think this is new?!" Forgive us, Lord, for our lazy complicity and averted gaze.

As discomfort pushed larger and larger numbers of people of faith into a deconstruction moment (because more and more Christians began to finally see their own faith tradition's complicity), I began to sit with a certain level of curiosity about how to relate to this shift. On the one hand, as a pastor in a progressive tradition racked considerably less by the influences of Christian nationalism and at least willing to speak up and organize for social justice (rather than dismiss social justice talk), I guess I was positioned to receive or walk alongside those deconstructing.

On the other hand, something inside of me said, "You don't know what you don't know." I tried to not step out and lead deconstruction conversations but rather join them and listen. And in particular, by the grace of God, I was given the chance to listen to African American voices.

I began following the creative and healing *Black Liturgies* of Cole Arthur Riley. I'm thankful to have started there, because those liturgies were comforting, constructive, real and needed as we all tried to adapt to the exigencies of pandemic.

Around this time, I was also discovering the work of adrienne maree brown. It took me a bit to begin to adapt myself both to her concepts and way of writing (this is about me not her, white men like me have been trained not to hear or listen well to such voices), but as I continued to sit with her 'emergent strategies' I found myself slowly shifting and transforming. Though not overtly a religious voice, nevertheless hers is a faithful voice. I trust her strategies and meditate on them regularly. I am trying to live them.

The principles of emergent strategy include:

- Small is good, small is all (The large is a reflection of the small).
- Change is constant (be like water).
- What you pay attention to grows.
- There is always a conversation in the room that only these people at this moment can have. Find it.
- There is always enough time for the right work.
- Move at the speed of trust (focus on critical connections more than critical mass—build the resilience by building the relationships).
- Never failure always a lesson.
- Less prep more presence.
- Trust the people (if you trust the people they become trust worthy).

But what has truly begun to consolidate my thinking is a new collection of reflections. The title may throw you off, if like me you hadn't (until the reading of the book) heard of "hush harbors." Short definition: a hush harbor was "a secluded informal structure, often built with tree branches, set in places away from masters so that slaves could meet to worship in private."

Liberating Church: A 21st Century Hush Harbor Manifesto gathers leaders of color who influence culture and work collectively to offer a vision for what faith community might begin to look like now considering all that has happened the past few years.

The authors engaged in ethnographic research at six ministries in Black communities in the South. They gathered the practices of these communities into eight "marks" of such communities: Ubuntu, Stay Woke, North Star, All God's Children Got Shoes, Steal Away, Sankofa, Joy Unspeakable, and Talking Book.

What I found remarkable while reading the book (and what literally kept me up until the morning hours pondering as I finished it) was the way it reclaims past practices of the Black church in antebellum America rather than deconstructing Christian nationalism.

I think deconstruction is important work, but it's also, like some previous movements like the emerging church movement, very Anglo. But if you attend to the voices in the Hush Harbor Manifesto, you hear them focused on reclaiming and retrieving examples of strength in their own history. As a white preacher in a predominately white church, it inspires me to spend more time looking to their manifesto and the history of the Black church as a guide rather than hyper-focusing on what to deconstruct in my own.

The manifesto points out:

> This moment [2020 and following] has revealed that the way we have organized churches produces consumers not disciples, acquaintances not deep friendships, behavior modifications not deep repentance, and volun-tourists not liberationists, flag-wavers not cross bearers, concubines of the state and not its conscience (*Liberating Church: A 21st Century Hush Harbor Manifesto*, edited by Brandon Wrencher and Venneikia Samantha Williams).

Then they quote Juan Luis Sgenudo, one of the great liberation theologians, who says, "If the very existence of the Church is meant to be leaven in the dough, salt in the meal, and light for all those who dwell in the human household, then ecclesial community must accept the obligations that derive from its essential function."

This framing is compelling. Our responsibility now in this moment as church is not to receive the revelation of the past few years and then say, "How can we get back to our comfort?" Our responsibility is to accept the obligations that derive from the essential function of the church as leaven, salt, light.

We are now forced to grapple with the need for egalitarian (often virtual) spaces rooted in mutuality. Now, more than ever, it seems we must make a radical turn. At our best, the Church brings unique gifts to this work. Think about it: we are a community of people who have been called into a life-long practice of repentance and transformation that demands that we face our frailties and faults while holding on to a sense of our belovedness. What would it look like for the church to be a leavening presence, aiding this work of transformation to take place on the personal, communal and political levels of our cities and world (*Liberating Church*, 3).

Howard Thurman says of the Hush Harbor movement, "By some amazing but vastly creative insight, they undertook the redemption of the religion that the master had profaned in their midst."

What I learn from this: it is unlikely that the masters (the profaners) will be able to redeem things themselves. For those of us still complicit in racist systems, it is incumbent upon us to listen to and learn from those who can retrieve and redeem what has been profaned. We literally don't know how to do it ourselves. But there are other communities who have been here before, many times, over the long haul. They recognize this as both a new and an old moment. We have ancestors who can guide us, and emerging communities sensitive to how God is moving in new ways.

Their way is not to reject the church, but to move differently. I'll conclude with one more quote from the *Hush Harbor Manifesto*:

> Church planting as a missionary strategy is how the religious right has spread white supremacist, hetero-patriarchal capitalism and the toxic Christian nationalism that upholds it. The Black Church and other social justice-oriented church traditions—especially those of us who consider ourselves radical and leftist—must deploy missional innovation as a cultural strategy for political and economic transformation in the US. This calls for an emergent liberate ecclesiology to be a movement that would organize new disciples not crowds, commit to base building not platform building, form sacred circles not elitist hierarchies, embody a radical politics not only seek to change politics in the public square.

FOR FURTHER READING

C. Arthur Riley. *Black Liturgies: Prayers, Poems, and Meditations for Staying Human*, Penguin 2024.

a. maree brown, *Emergent Strategy: Shaping Changing, Changing World*, AK Press, 2017.

THE FUTURE OF THE CHURCH: THOUGHTS ON NEW MEDIA

W hy, when the church thinks about the future, does it focus on technology? Why does popular culture also equate the future with a technological future, and focus on new technologies as a renewed hope for transition or a cause of decline?

The answer is twofold. As illustrated in *Mediating Faith: Faith Formation For a Transmedia Era*, partially it's simply because we sometimes confuse new media with *the effect of the transition* to new media. Precisely because it is new it garners more of our attention.

However, the second reason is more dismal: the church has largely capitulated to a vision of the future encompassed entirely by the capitalist frame, and so it (mostly) can't imagine any (hopeful) future other than one that is mediated by new technology.

Take, as a recent prominent example, TryTank's "Faith in the Future" video for the Episcopal Church. If you have ten minutes, you can watch it at TryTank's web site. If you don't have time for the video, the narrator makes three suggestions based on trends for what the future of the church might be. They are:

- *Distributed church: small micro-churches gathering all over*
- *Authentic do-it-yourself spirituality: basically, an app where you can access all kinds of theology*
- *Blended reality experiences: by which he means Oculus and other VR resources*

Now, I don't want to be too hard on this video or the narrator of it, but if you think about what the church *is*, you can see where these are all somewhat problematic proposals for the *future* of the church. I don't mean that these aren't trends. They certainly are. But they're only trends in media and mediation, not a vision for the future of *the church*.

In the video, the narrator points out that younger generations have looked at the church and found it wanting, and then have organized for social justice in ways that are very aligned with ... the church. And he's right. There's more of a relationship between the biblical prophets and Christian theology and a humanist progressive vision for the commons than many disconnected from religion may be aware.

And it might be that skillful use of new media might help

bridge the divide between a secularizing younger generation and an aging church.

However, if we want to look at trends and project what the future of the church might be in 2032, as the video attempts, we should keep in mind that the vision in the video is very constrained by a) bourgeois values, and b) capitalism.

It's doubtful unhoused people (many of whom are Christian) hope for a future church that allows for more mediated experiences through virtual reality devices. The future of the church for an unhoused person would be a church that provides housing.

Similarly, although it's certainly true that small groups have always and will continue to meet with intentionality, those micro-communities need to be connected to larger ecclesial institutions, if they are to offer the kind of solace in community and challenge in the polis we've come to value from progressive church.

Finally, if church leaders think that if they just create the right app to put great spiritual resources at the fingertips of new media users, perhaps they are forgetting *this already exists.*

The issue isn't that people don't have liberation theology or queer theology or eco-feminist theology at their fingertips. They do. Technology is already set up to provide access to all these theological resources in text, audio, video and more. Despite Marshall McLuhan's idea that *the medium is the message,* the medium is not the content of the message itself. One would hope all sermons in 2032 won't be *about* virtual reality devices or apps.

Remember (sorry, brief digression) that when McLuhan's book came out the printer accidentally gave the book the title *The Medium Is the Massage*, and McLuhan liked it so much he kept it that way. McLuhan's insight into the effects of new media is that media is neither simply the vehicle through which the message is delivered, nor is the medium a replacement for the message, but rather there is an effect, a way in which the medium "massages" the messages, with some media more subtly doing so than others (even to the point where some media become extensions of the human themselves—the written word may be an example).

If we are going to ask ourselves about the *future of the church*, we would do better to acknowledge virtual reality, or distributed forms of communication, network effects, democratized access to theological and sacramental resources, all *may* impact how the church in the future functions, and it's also the case almost all of the new media arising now is increasingly conformed to a vision for the future captive to the hegemony of capitalism.

The church can't imagine future church outside of these new media because the church, together with much of the rest of the world, can't imagine an alternative to capitalism.

I've always appreciated Ursula K. LeGuin's comments at her acceptance speech in 2014 for Distinguished Contribution to American Letters:

> We live in capitalism. Its power seems inescapable. So did the divine right of kings. Any human power can be resisted and

changed by human beings. Resistance and change often begin in art, and very often in our art, the art of words.

Why, we might ask, would the church surrender to capitalism? Why would it allow its vision for the future to be (almost) entirely populated by the capitalist vision? We know, for example, this is why many progressive Christians are so adamantly progressive—we still hold out for an alternative to capitalism. Many of us do so by imagining along the lines of democratic socialism, even if we also recognize that socialism, though closer to the kin-dom of God, is still not the coming kin-dom.

Nevertheless, if I were going to cast a vision for 2032 and invite all the readers of this book to envision the church of 2032, I'd invite us to at least try to hope for a future not constrained by the straitjacket of the current hegemonic economic system or the perils of nationalism.

If we are looking for trend-lines, I'd rather focus on trends I see happening in the church that carry synergy with the trend-lines of social justice movements the world over. If you ask me, what are the top three things I envision for the church of 2032 as a progressive pastor, I'd say:

- The church overcomes the heresy of national borders and welcomes the stranger, everywhere.
- The church resists the modern Caesar, capitalism, and instead of capitulating, begins practicing an alternative economy, one especially focused on creation care.

- The church takes its sacraments literally, and so ensures everyone has a glass of clean water, everyone has food, and by analogy, pours itself out for the poor because it discovers God in their midst.

I imagine distributed church, authentic do-it-yourself church, and even blended reality experiences *may* play a role in the church moving toward that future. But the future I've outlined has as its inspiration not a rapacious economic system or the most recent new media innovations, but rather the coming Spirit of God.

FOR FURTHER READING
C. Schnekloth, *Mediating Faith: Faith Formation in a Trans-Media Era*, Fortress Press, 2014.

THE ANXIETY OF CHRISTIAN MISSION/EVANGELISM

That which is descriptively true need not be prescriptive. Take the spread of Christianity. Just because it has continually grown as a faith across the globe doesn't necessarily mean it should or must.

Here's the basic thesis: faith in Christ spread in the early church as a word of promise and hope to many kinds of beleaguered communities. However, when the church heedlessly interprets the natural spread of "good news" as a prescription, as command or demand, it corrupts the very message it found so naturally missional.

Consider an analogy: when Taylor Swift tickets go on sale, the news of the opportunity to see her in concert spreads incredibly quickly. There's a natural vitality to the spread of certain kinds of news based on their appeal. If you like something you tell your friends about it, especially if you think they'll get joy out of it also.

But imagine if the fan-base turned what is descriptively true (that they love to listen to and share Taylor's music) into command (we must listen to her music and get others to listen to it also). That would be a problem, right? If all Taylor Swift fans suddenly felt that anyone who didn't listen to Taylor Swift was lost, lacking hope of real life, etc. that would be ... bad.

And yet this is precisely how many Christians have approached mission and evangelism, as if they share the good news not out of delight, but because they are required to spread it by the direct commands of Jesus *and* if they don't spread it those who haven't heard it yet will be damned, live hopeless lives, etc.

In this understanding of evangelism/mission, good news becomes law. In this understanding of the good news, it takes on a supremacist tone that brooks no rivals: Christianity becomes totalitarian. If you are a Christian, you have to spread it to others: if you haven't become a Christian yet you have to accept it or be irredeemably lost.

What a bunch of crap.

Let's try to think Christian mission/evangelism in a different way, less totalitarian, less hegemonic, less legalistic, more free and mutual. What might that entail?

Let's start with the posture of Jesus himself. When we look at the life of Jesus, we see how relaxed he was in terms of "global mission." Although he was clearly committed to his mission (he was willing to die for it) what he didn't do was use his divinity or any other powers or strategies to "reach" the whole world or "demand" fealty. In fact, to a considerable degree he did the opposite of these two things. He stayed pretty close to home and only reluctantly went down to Jerusalem at the right time and understood his work to be especially related to bringing a message of wholeness and healing to his own people, always open to sharing that message "accidentally" with those outside Israel he encountered on the way.

It would be an entire analysis to page, moment by moment, through the entire ministry of Christ, but it doesn't take long reviewing his life to note how gently evangelical and non-colonial it was. He rarely if ever challenged or called into question the beliefs or culture of those outside of Israel; the biggest theological challenges he made were to those already part of the religious system.

Of course, there is that one verse at the end of the gospel of Matthew, on which the evangelical impulse of Christianity has placed such heavy emphasis—the Great Commission. But it's notable how distinct those verses are from the rest of Matthew and the gospels more generally.

We can also take as further example some religious traditions who are quite neighborly with Christianity but far less evangelical. I think here of Buddhist traditions, as well as many other non-Christian faiths. These neighbors of ours are willing to share their insights, philosophies, traditions with others but with a lot less of the anxiety inherent in the anxious posture of Christian mission. It's almost as if their sense of self-identity is less wrapped up in securing their identity by getting everyone else to be like them.

Finally, consider those forms of Christian mission that are more closely connected to Christ himself ... that is to say, Christological understandings of mission/evangelism.

A wonderful centering concept is a term that originates in the work of Bonhoeffer and von Balthasar, that of *stellvertretung*. Sometimes this is translated as "representation," but can also be translated as "place-sharing." The classic notion common in Christian circles is that Christ "takes our place" as regards the punishment for sin. But more generally speaking, the emphasis is on God in Christ becoming fully human so that we might share in God's place. Christ becomes human so that humans might become divine.

If this place-sharing (*stellvertretung*) is a model for Christian mission/evangelism, it offers an entirely different posture for the Christian's way of sharing "good news" in the world. It inspires us to enter the space of the neighbor, to imagine ourselves in the neighbor's place, with a mutual invitation for our neighbors to imagine themselves into our place.

This is why interfaith hospitality, openness to sharing with one another across religious traditions, is ultimately a more faithful form of mission than a posture of demanded evangelism and expected conversion. In the same way that God saw enough value in becoming human to become fully human, you might say the Christian is invited to become fully their neighbor, without remainder.

Rather than anxiously hoping our neighbors might become

like us, we love our neighbors enough to become more like them. A Christian may become more Christian by deepening their understanding of and connection to the religions of others (even the non-religious, the atheists). In such a relationship, a Christian can still share why it is Christ's place-sharing with them has been so profoundly influential in their lives, but they do so freely, without demand or expectation.

What this can inspire in progressive Christians is a radical new openness to faith-sharing. Many progressive Christians have attended to post-colonial thinking and the dangers of totalitarianism. We are rightly reluctant to repeat the harm of Christian mission of the colonial sort. However, if faith-sharing has to do with place-sharing, it then replaces "converting the other" with "we grow in mutual inter-relationship with the other," each side taking responsibility for what that growth looks like.

On a practical level, this kind of posture allows our congregation to share in real friendship with interfaith communities. Over time, when the Islamic Center or the synagogue or the Buddhist community sees our Christian community is genuinely interested in mutuality, partnerships, interfaith learning, then their worries about being evangelized (something very common in the South with the dominance of Southern Baptist evangelism practices), a kind of relaxed shared mission can arise. The results of these kinds of interfaith connections can be remarkable and glorious.

And they cannot happen, ever, if the Christian starts from

the posture of "these people of another religious tradition lack something we have and it's our job to give it to them."

It can happen when we begin from the posture of "we can each grow in our own traditions by deepening our understand of and friendship with those of other traditions."

FOR FURTHER READING

B. Konkol, *Mission as Accompaniment: A Response to Mechanistic Dehumanization*, Fortress Press, 2017.

MUTUAL AID

I was raised in a Christian culture that idealized charity and mission trips. Our church, solidly middle class, was one of those large churches before there were mega-churches. When we helped people, which we did often, it was very much a patron-client model. As in:

- Our youth group is going to the soup kitchen to feed the hungry
- We are taking a group on a mission trip to help a blighted community two states away
- We are donating some funds out of our excess to the needs of people across the world who can't afford X, Y, or Z

As I try to think back on this early formation, it occurs to me I was very rarely if ever taught that I was the hungry, the blighted community, or the needy. I was taught instead that I had so very much, and it was the Christian thing to do to give from the overflowing cup of blessings I had received.

What we especially NEVER did was go meet the racially and economically OTHER just down the hill by the river and join those communities in Christian mission. I was supposed to have compassion ON the poor. I was not trained to see myself in solidarity WITH the poor. And I was never taught to consider my/our complicity in the systems that made people poor in the first place.

I think I continued in the charity mindset until my early 20s, around the time our denomination published a rather remarkable statement on Christian mission as accompaniment. This model, focused on how global churches relate to one another, focuses on "the mutual respect of the churches that are in relationship, the companions. The conversation is no longer between a giver and a receiver, but between churches, all of which have gifts to give and to receive."

I was already experiencing mission as accompaniment in my work as an ELCA missionary in eastern Slovakia. I was learning as a teacher that I had gifts to share, as well as much to learn, and that Christian mission could be deeply reciprocal rather than patronizing. I was also getting my first exposure to the eastern bloc, which had itself loomed large in my imagination as the system the west "opposed." I was a Cold War kid and crossing that no-longer existing wall did some thawing.

However, once you have been trained in the charity mindset, it's a lifelong journey shifting to an alternative way. Anti-charity work is like anti-racism work, it's something that can with intentionality be done. A simple example: In 2020, when the Marshallese community was experiencing especially tragic outcomes from COVID-19, I went into my normal charity mode. And indeed, early in our planning there really was a dynamic of "we have a need, and you have the resources." However, because I had a long-standing friendship with Albious Latior, a leader in that community, we leaned on our relationship to discover together how to minister as Christians.

We discovered along the way needs on both sides: a need to share resources, a need to tell the story locally and nationally, culturally appropriate ways Marshallese "gift-back." Certainly, we've never perfectly disentangled ourselves from the charity mindset, but inasmuch as possible we've placed the Marshallese community itself in the driver's seat for our way of accompanying. I would add, notice also how this accompaniment model of ministry leans toward the local. Rather than raising funds to send missionaries far away, we have developed a relationship between different people groups right here in Northwest Arkansas.

Around the same time, we were developing this partnership, a Facebook group emerged online titled Y'ALLIDARITY — NWA Mutual Aid. The description: "NWA Mutual Aid is a volunteer collective that exists to help build resilient communities through organizing collaborative efforts, connecting folks to existing local resources, and providing a space for the community to connect and exchange support."

I'm going to be vulnerable here and admit I'd never heard of "mutual aid" prior to the launch of this Facebook group. I'd seen t-shirts reading "Y'allidarity." They're kind of common among those of us who are socialists in the South. But not "mutual aid." And actually, for a month or two I thought "mutual aid" was a label they'd created themselves. It was even more recently I learned it had a longer pedigree, in fact all the way back to the 19th century debates around evolution and social Darwinism.

One of the best things you can do right now, if like me mutual aid is a new concept, is pause and read about mutual aid over at Wikipedia. Do it! Wikipedia is a kind of model of mutual aid, so it's the perfect place to learn more. One thing you learn right away: mutual aid has a very long pedigree, traced all the way back to an anarchist philosopher, Peter Kropotkin, who argued that cooperation rather than competition was the driving force for evolution.

More recent "anarchists" have continued reflecting on mutual aid, and one of the most accessible, and short, books is Dean Spade's *Mutual Aid: Building Solidarity During This Crisis*. Here's the BIG difference between mutual aid and charity. There are two parts. First, mutual aid is about responding in community, creating innovative ways to share resources and support vulnerable neighbors. *It's survival work.*

But mutual aid conjoins meeting basic needs *with social movements demanding transformative change.* Combining aid with social movements demanding change: that was definitely NOT on the agenda of middle-class churches when I was growing up, and it's STILL not on the agenda of most churches yet today. I know a lot of churches that feed people. I know very few churches that organize movements aiming for a basic income for everyone. I know a lot of churches that give out a bit of cash assistance. I know of very few churches that attempt to deconstruct rich foundations so wealth stops being doled out in tiny doses by the elite.

Perhaps the pandemic has facilitated the kinds of shifts we really need right now away from patronizing charity. Solidarity not charity! We need not just aid but transformation toward collective action.

There's a great quote toward the end of Dean Spade's book, taken from the document Mutual Aid Disaster Relief.

The only thing that keeps those in power in that position is the illusion of our powerlessness. A moment of freedom and connection can undo a lifetime of social conditioning and scatter seeds in a thousand directions.

I continually ask myself this question: why are so many Christian communities willing to throw themselves into forms of charity, especially ones they perceive as mostly apolitical, but they won't lead or join social movements demanding transformative change? Is it possible they feel powerless? Or are they so in thrall to middle class captivity they can't see that transformative change is at the heart of the gospel, not ancillary to it?

What I especially love about mutual aid is its secularity. My previous term for this, accompaniment, as useful as it is in church contexts, was developed in and by a Christian church. Mutual aid is the work of everyone. It's a grassroots term, a concept from down below, an-archist in the literal sense of that term. Progressive Christians lean in to learning from the mutual aid folks, because often the most faithful concepts are elevated and practiced not in the churches, but in the inspiring communities the churches are invited to join. This also is part of the awareness of "progressive church."

FOR FURTHER READING
D. Spade, *Mutual Aid: Building Solidarity During This Crisis,* Verso, 2020.

PROGRESSIVE CHRISTIANS IN DAILY LIFE

L et's begin by acknowledging that in terms of the total number of hours available to us in any given week, almost none of them, for most people, are spent at church. Most of the time most of us are at home or work or school or at the store. As a pastor, I'm under no illusion that church as hub-of-all-things-social is still the paradigm. That's kind of an "America of the 1950s" thing. Yes, some people really used to conduct almost all their social gathering at church, and some small sub-cultures still do. But in the spring of 2022 cell phone data indicates only 5% of Americans gather weekly on their primary day of worship, and on any given week only about 45 million are in a place of worship. That's about 12%.

Statistically this means if you're affiliated with a progressive church and value, it highly and contribute to it generously, you're still not there in the building all that often. For this post,

I'm going to take that as a given, and ponder a vision for how to do progressive church life beyond the church walls.

Here's an example:

For the past few years, our congregation has deepened its participation in International Trans Day of Visibility. Post-pandemic 2022 was the first opportunity organizers had had in a couple of years to host the event in person. A local community center generously offered space and so for a Saturday in March the trans community had a lecture hall, meeting rooms, and even the swimming pool available for their use.

When I arrived at the event and scanned the lecture hall where the first plenary would take place, I started ticking off on my hand the number of people in the room who were affiliated with our congregation. It was a not insignificant percentage. Two of the panelists were members. A third panelist, though not a member, was a volunteer at our Queer Camp the summer prior. And in the audience were many attendees, trans and allies. Our people hadn't arrived en bloc, and there was not a concerted push within the congregation to attend the day of visibility together. It just happened naturally (as a byproduct of who we are as a church) that support of the trans community is integral to our congregational commitments. As a social justice organizing church some of our people follow the spiritual practice of *showing up*.

When I'm at events like this, and see our church community there, I'm reminded of all the little parables Jesus taught concerning the impact of small things. One of the shortest is the parable of the leaven:

And again, he said, "To what shall I compare the kingdom of God? It is like leaven that a woman took and hid in three measures of flour, until it was all leavened." (Luke 13:20-21)

This is one reason progressive Christianity rarely makes the headlines and seldom sits in seats of power. It hides and leavens. A basic commitment of progressivism is solidarity with the poor and minoritized, those social groups displaced to the margins of society. Because progressive Christianity often empties itself in such solidarity, it typically fails to consolidate power at the center of society.

Yet Jesus envisions in his parable of the kin-dom of God that such self-emptying and hiding leavens everything. Going small and weak is movement closer to the ways of God in Christ.

You might ask yourself now how you as an everyday progressive Christian, busy with the commitments of daily life, like work and family, can most faithfully hide as leaven. And here I have two basic suggestions:

1. Look for the opportunities right where you are.
2. If you're looking for a more significant opportunity, choose the one that is divestment for you and presence with the poor.

OPPORTUNITIES RIGHT WHERE YOU ARE

Sometimes we are enamored of the grand gesture. We become convinced it is only the truly committed, or those with high ideals and radical practice, who can truly exemplify progressive Christian values. But really the shifts that can occur in our society that move us in progressive directions happen through a blend of small individual actions and steady community organizing.

A small individual action: cancel one streaming service and commit that much monthly to your local progressive church (or movement) instead.

Another small individual action: bike or carpool to church. Ideally, give someone a ride who doesn't have their own transportation.

Yet another small individual action: take one hour you'd otherwise spend doom-scrolling and instead draft one letter to the editor for your local newspaper.

A family action: team up with another family and practice the art of *showing up*. March in a pride parade, visit an ethnic or interfaith community in your neighborhood, take a concrete physical presence action aligned with your progressive values.

DIVEST AND PRACTICE SOLIDARITY

Progressive Christianity offers a vision for the future that is joyous and just. Along the way, those committed to living into that vision will have to make some sacrifices. One of the biggest sacrifices will likely be guilt by affiliation. Inevitably your co-workers and friends will relate to you differently or even distance themselves from you if you practice real solidarity with communities of the poor and marginalized.

Divestment and solidarity begin with really listening to such communities and then taking their lead. A frequent liberal mistake (I have made this mistake often) is to identify *for* the poor what they really need from me in terms of solidarity. In this liberal model, I put myself in the position of patron who can help a poor client with their needs.

I've come to appreciate and value the concept of mutual aid. In mutual aid, we recognize that we all need help, and have gifts to share with each other. As just one example, take The Little Free Pantry, a movement founded on our church driveway. A Little Free Pantry is just a box. You can put stuff in it, you can take stuff from it. You can meet your need to give. Someone else can meet their need by taking what you have given.

If you are lending your voice and advocacy to an issue, it's good to keep in mind the basic mantra, "Nothing about us without us." If you do write that letter to the editor, or post an opinion on social media, or stand outside with a sign, make sure you've listened long enough to know you are aligning with the voices of the impacted communities. Listening in solidarity with the subaltern before acting is a form of divestment, because it means, particularly for those of us with voice and resources, that we must begin from a position of vulnerability and not-knowing. We may discover while listening that the needs of the community are quite different from the ones we had supposed, and the strategies for change desired by the community uncomfortable to our own sensibilities.

I really do believe, finally, that progressive Christianity is harder to perceive in our world and culture because it functions synthetically in consonance with culture rather than opposite to it. This is particularly true in relationship to humanist values. There is quite a bit of alignment between the humanism that has shaped some of our greatest civic institutions and the progressive understanding of Christianity.

Nikolai Grundtvig, a leading Lutheran theologian and early developer of public education, spoke of this as a commitment to "human first, then Christian."

Where progressives part ways with culture is particularly those aspects of culture that more conservative modes of Christianity attempt to align with. Progressives are more "Christ against culture" when it comes to nationalism, the dominance of capitalism, paternalism, etc.

In the everyday world progressive Christianity is synthesized most naturally with aspects of culture that are perceived as secularizing (socialism in particular) but then opposed to or against aspects of culture that are widely tacitly accepted as natural by modern Christianity.

This puts progressive Christians in some very odd spaces when it comes to everyday life, not least of which is their posture toward participation in the life of the church itself. Returning to the example of the Trans Day of Visibility, I think the average progressive Christian attending that event may not think of themselves as attending *as* a Christian. They're just participating as a good neighbor, as a good human.

I don't know if you call this way of being sublimation, or something else, but I do think it goes a long way toward helping all of us understand what it means for a progressive Christian to live in the everyday, which is not generally at war with the wider culture or carrying the understanding of being oppressed by it, but rather feeling at war with specifically the very parts of the culture most wedded to the dominant forms of Christianity— the market and the state.

That's quite a conundrum, and it's both odd and illustrative that I have to end up writing about that when talking about progressive Christians in everyday life.

FOR FURTHER READING

D. Kaden, *Christianity In Blue: How the Bible, History, Philosophy, and Theology Shape Progressive Identity*, Fortress Press, 2021.

APPENDIX I

PROGRESSIVE CHURCH AS EXEMPLIFIED IN TWO MONTHS OF "SHORT" MEDIA POSTS

Each of the following was originally a "short" post on Facebook, and hopefully exemplifies an ongoing progressive church social media approach ...

NOVEMBER 10TH, 2022

A Dozen Lesser-Known Facts About Worship At GSLC:
1. For the last year we've been reading from womanist Old Testament scholar Wil Gafney's "Women's Lectionary," which includes using "she/her" for God when translating the Psalms.

2. Although we've typically recited the Apostles' or Nicene Creed in worship, in the new year we'll begin a cycle of reciting other creeds, especially the Magnificat (Advent), the Beatitudes

(Lent), the Prayer of St. Francis (Easter), and maybe if we're feeling radical Dorothee Soelle's Credo or our own version of it.

3. In December we return to using the Revised Common Lectionary, a three-year cycle of readings from Scripture (one from Old Testament, one from the epistles, one from the Psalms, one from the gospels) that we share with thousands of churches across the world. 2022-2023 is Year A, the year of Matthew.

4. We tend not to do a lot of "me and my boyfriend Jesus" songs and try to weave more social justice songs into our worship. Except sometimes we do still sing the boyfriend songs because it's kind of fun to consider Jesus as boyfriend.

5. We follow a "liturgy" or "ordo," which means a fixed order of worship that includes a gathering rite, lessons from Scripture and a sermon on them, then Communion, and a sending. Although we also love "from the heart" prayers and worship, we believe that if you memorize something you know it "by heart."

6. We have an organ AND a praise band every Sunday, so it's like you're at a concert with Creedence Clearwater Revival AND Yo-Yo Ma.

7. Because the acolytes have really gotten into it most Sundays you receive communion from kids. They're good at it, and sometimes race to see who serves what. Anyone can receive communion at our church. That includes all children, any age.

8. We only serve gluten-free bread and juice because why divide the meal and exclude those with a gluten-intolerance or

issues with alcohol? Plus gluten-free bread is tasty, and so is juice.

9. Our Sunday school team has begun doing their program during worship, exiting at the lessons and returning in time for communion. This gives the chance for small children to hear the gospel at a developmentally appropriate level, but still learn most parts of the liturgy.

10. You want to become a member? Members are as members do, so come and be active. Subscribe to our e-mail and get us your contact info. We offer a spiritual program during the Lenten season (spring/Easter) that culminates in an affirmation of baptism service or baptisms at the Easter Vigil (the Saturday evening of Easter weekend).

11. We started a new practice post-pandemic that has really taken off. It's the mutual consolation of the saints, and basically, we invite people at the conclusion of worship to go meet someone new and ask them, genuinely, how things are with their soul. It's become a powerful way for the community to care for each other.

12. LGBTQIA+ folks not only participate in worship but lead it. A significant portion of our worship and preaching team is LGBTQIA.

NOVEMBER 9TH

On Creating Shelter for Unsheltered Families in NWA and Turning Our Church into a Shelter for LGBTQIA Youth and Young Adults

As a congregation the past few years we have become hyper aware of the multiple pressures resulting in increased houselessness in our community.

During the pandemic we helped countless households stay in their apartments or homes, assisting where we could with rent and utilities, and advocating for greater protections for renters.

As we have shifted to this new phase in the crisis with housing and shelter, I've been pondering our current strategies. I know, for example, that the local municipal housing program is maxed out and no longer accepting applications. The shelters are full. So is the domestic abuse shelter.

As we are preparing for winter, some local organizations are teaming up to provide emergency low-barrier shelter if temperatures go below 15 degrees (this is something you can volunteer to help with).

But this is not nearly enough. We have a crisis in our community that will only get worse as rents sky-rocket. In the past week I've had resource folks from more than one of these orgs just come and visit at my office and express their frustration and exhaustion.

As a socialist I wish the state and federal governments simply provided shelter for everyone. That would be the best solution. But that is unlikely to happen in our area because our government mostly doesn't care about the poor and often simply blames them.

Similarly, none of the biggest grant-giving organizations in our area prioritize housing on their list of funding targets.

In other words, at the meta-level our housing crisis is intractable and unlikely to be addressed, at least in the short-term, by large systemic measures.

So, I've been sitting around thinking about "the next right thing." And I know what it is.

In January I'm working to bring representatives from Family Promise to Northwest Arkansas to look at forming a chapter in our area. Family Promise organizes churches to provide emergency shelter for unhoused families. The focus is on families with children.

This is a gap in our community—no shelter for unhoused families.

The other next right thing is for us to open some of our church space specifically for a LGBTQIA+ young adult shelter. [As of the publication of this book we currently house four.] This is something we've been pondering for a while, but as I talk with case workers at area shelters, and talk with staff at the schools, I realize this is a growing issue.

My friend Heidi Neumark pastors a church in Manhattan that provides shelter for LGBTQIA+ young people like this. She says many, perhaps a majority, come to Manhattan from the South. So, developing a resource in Arkansas makes sense.

In December I'll be hosting a Zoom conversation with Heidi and their social worker Wendy. I'm happy to include all those interested in that Zoom call. Just let me know.

It will take multiple steps to get from point A to point B in this plan. However, I'm convinced that our little congregation can be part of the solution. I'm also convinced (because I drive around and see all the churches) that we have more than enough buildings and more than enough people to provide better shelter.

And if any of those working at the big foundations want to have a conversation and realign priorities so we buy just a few less Rothko's and build a few more shelters, please consider this the prod into that conversation.

NOVEMBER 6TH

The other day a friend told me they were a little tired of their pastors always saying that people needed to come back to church. This friend attends a large church here in Fayetteville. They liked something I'd said recently in a post, "If you just drive through the church parking lot Sunday morning and then feel you need to leave, that's fine. Consider it a test run."

I think a lot of us church people are struggling to say out loud what has really happened in these last three years. There may even be a bit of shame in it all ... combined with a bit of relief when we learn we really are (at least many of us) going through the same thing ... because when I finally do talk with colleagues about their churches post-pandemic, I hear very similar stories across the country.

First, they experienced a lot of change. In some ways it felt like a turn-over.

Second, overall worship attendance in person on Sunday mornings is down around 1/4 to 1/3 from where it was.

I've heard this from Baptist pastors, Episcopalian priests,

various Lutherans, etc. The only exception seems to be very rural churches.

What feels discombobulating (and I don't think I'm alone in this) is that many of those who haven't "come back" also haven't clarified their intentions. Many if not most of our church members still donate. They still follow church life on social media, stay connected with fellow members, etc. If I run into parishioners at the grocery store or on the trail, they emphatically and quickly say they mean to get back to church.

But ...

The stories of why people aren't back yet are so varied. Some discovered that as an introvert it was simply far more relaxing to stay home Sunday morning and watch service online. Others discovered they just didn't need church that much. Still others started attending during the pandemic because they DID need church that much.

Overall, there's just a level of exhaustion among everyone, and church is one of the spaces that feels "optional" and therefore the one from which folks take a break for rest.

On the other hand, it's also just about the delay of return. Many members of our church who haven't been inside the church for over two years are still showing up on Sundays, and sometimes even stating they feel like the Prodigal returning.

At the same time, there are so many new faces each week it's hard to keep up. We're not a big congregation but I bet we average 10-20 new visitors every Sunday.

There appears to be a general spiritual search happening, in many directions all at once.

I'm trying to figure out how to stop thinking about the topic, and certainly not send out any more letters or give out any messages that just sound like the pastor complaining everyone needs to come back.

I know I can't get my congregation to DO any particular thing through a concerted effort. If I could, then the messages and invites and calls I've made already would have resulted in a big sweeping return. They haven't. And that's fine. I shouldn't assume I have such a magic touch.

What I can tell you is how it feels to gather each Sunday morning with this much change.

What it feels like is vulnerable.

What it feels like is a moderate level of confusing. Like, since people really do know precisely how much of an impact our little church had and continues to have helping neighbors during the pandemic and after, how come people don't give of their time and resources here as freely as they give to football and rock concerts?

What it also feels like is living in a time of glorious emergence. Those who are present really want to be present. They're all in. We introduced a time at the end of the service this fall inviting everyone to meet someone new and really ask each other how they're doing, and now there's a period of about 20 minutes or more at the conclusion of worship of what we call the "mutual consolation of the saints," and I think easily over half of people really stay and really talk and it's noisy. In a good "people loving their neighbors" kind of way.

That's what you miss if you aren't there in person. You miss the serendipity of those encounters and what might emerge. That's what's poignant to me.

But I also get what's attractive about sleeping in, catching up on the house-cleaning you couldn't get do during the week, raking all the leaves. The demands of everyday life in 2022 are substantial.

I really believe a part of moving faithfully in the world is having a true picture of it. What I'm offering here is a true picture of why I can't stop wishing folks would come back to church in greater numbers while also expressing understanding and sympathy for why they don't.

All that being said, more and more I do feel a calm coming over me each week. I walk to church most Sundays, and there just isn't this weight. It feels like we are being who we are called to be as a church. Living the mantra: "We are who we are now." As adrienne maree brown says in *Emergent Strategy*, "Small is good. Small is all."

ALSO NOVEMBER 6TH

This is your daily reminder that Moms for Liberty is a hate group and is targeting our school board and teaching staff and students with bullying and bigoted tactics on a daily basis.

NOVEMBER 1ST

Today I'm subbing in Child Development and Growth. Once again, a reminder the kids are alright.

The sub office said they have 45 teachers out today, and as of 8:30 am as classes were starting there were still 13 spots unfilled. In practice this means classes are regularly being combined, or students are placed in hallway study areas with one adult supervising multiple classes in a kind of holding pattern.

It also means teachers are regularly giving up needed prep hours to sub for one another.

One of the biggest concerns I have is the school district decreased pay for subs between last school year and this one by about 20%. Yes, by 20%. When there is a shortage of subs and inflation.

As we go into winter and flu season, I have concern of even more severe shortage of subs. I also have real justice concerns that those supporting our schools as subs are paid less per hour than what most high schoolers make when hired for their first jobs.

We can do better.

OCTOBER 30TH

I often wish I could interpret to the wider world, conservative Christians and really everyone, why it is that holding fun parties like Nightmare Before Gay Christmas is healing work.

Perhaps this will help: tonight, a student from the University of Arkansas television came out and wanted to interview us about being being an affirming congregation. It took them a while just to cross the threshold into the building. It took a lot more questions for them to begin to process how different it really is. They were so nervous. Lots of religious trauma.

Because what we had was an entire building full of queer kids (plus a group playing DnD) who just felt safe, as themselves. And this university student had never seen that, and wondered why he couldn't find it on campus.

I sure wish he could. We try. It's hard competing with bigoted churches whose annual budgets are 30-40 times ours. But I'm glad at least that our little party with the fog machine and great costumes and a little too much sugar and some tarot reading in the back corner could be a balm and sign of hope for him.

OCTOBER 24TH

I'm entirely fascinated by the energy we are gathering for a "service" here at church that isn't specifically Christian but instead focuses on bodily practices and meal-sharing.

As we have gathered in small groups to brainstorm and imagine, the shape of the service has coalesced around two simple practices: opening with spiritual practices that are movement oriented (sitting, meditation, stretching, fascia work, etc.) and then moving into a meal with some facilitated conversation.

Our next meeting of the core team that will coordinate these services is this Wednesday at 6:30 p.m., and we will likely begin the Wednesday after Thanksgiving. If the format interests you, you're welcome to connect with the core team and planning.

So, here's the part I find fascinating: churches have typically hosted worship for "believers" and so a lot of worship has included prayers, sermons, hymns, and creeds that make sense if the assumption is that everyone "believes" approximately the same thing and is willing to confess those beliefs together.

If you don't believe those things, you don't tend to want to join such gatherings.

And yet ... here we have many folks who don't necessarily believe all the things but still wish to gather in meaningful community that is "Christian adjacent."

Historically, the church has hosted this kind of space as a time for inquiry. I think they used to call it a "seeker" service. But those services were still "doctrinal."

However, Christianity, much like other faith traditions, has a wide set of embodied practices that do not have to be explicitly tied to any creed. Meditation and silence. Meal-sharing and service. So, although it has never occurred to me to have a "non-Christian" service at a Christian church, I can see why it makes sense, and why in particular although it may look a lot like traditions like Unitarian Universalist that are open and non-creed specific, nevertheless in another way it is a kind of interfaith practice that arises out of a peculiar way of being Christian.

I like to think of it as Being Human, which I think is also what we'll call the gatherings. Our church finds a lot of ways to be human together with people of other faiths or no faith at all, and we want to find ways to spend time together, know ourselves and one another better, and there are ways to do this.

The central point: you can have a "service" that doesn't lead to conversion or focus on conversion in a particular direction or to just one faith. You can gather in ways that cultivate multi-faith belonging, that hold space for many faiths or even those pushed away by faiths, and there's a gentle center to all of that we can refrain from naming, in the same way our tradition sometimes refrains from naming "The Name."

OCTOBER 22

General notes for worshipping at GSLC:

You can dress how you want.

The Psalms refer to God as She/Her.

Right now we just have the one 10 am service but we're launching a Wednesday service in December.

There are often interjections.

There's a band AND an organ and choir.

Currently there's children's church kids go out during lessons and sermon and return for communion.

We don't print bulletins. There's a screen and a QR code.

You can bring your recycling (the stuff Sam's Club takes). you can also fill the Friendly Fridge and the Little Free Pantry.

There are a lot of rainbows.

There's a public labyrinth and Gaga ball pit.

If you drive through the parking lot and then decide you just can't come in that's fine too. Test runs are cool. And there's a livestream.

OCTOBER 16TH

I've now served as pastor of Good Shepherd Lutheran Church for 12 years.

Can't say that I ever imagined serving in one congregation for this long.

I also can't say that I ever thought I would love it so much.

Today as I was driving across Missouri returning from marching band competition, I had the chance to listen to the live stream of worship back at home.

It was a remarkable experience.

I had this major concern in the middle of my ministry at GSLC, right after the split over same-gender marriage in 2014. At that time there was a hyper focus on my leadership as the pastor of the congregation. To many who left the congregation I was the villain and to many who stayed I was the hero.

The reality: I was neither. I simply took one specific step, a hard one, and then accepted the costs whatever those were going to be.

Mostly I'm just a pastor with my own idiosyncrasies trying to be faithful.

Nevertheless, a lot of the congregational identity was carried by my identity as pastor through that split because honestly, the church was made up of the people who decided to stay when others tried to vote me out.

Which brings me back to listening to the service today over the live stream. I really was in awe. This is a people who know who they are. Ted our longtime drummer and musician led the liturgy and presided at the Eucharist. Nanci, a member of our preaching team, delivered the sermon. We hosted a wonderful amalgam of band and bells and choir.

This whole community of people can very readily and wonderfully do the church thing while I'm off for a weekend helping with my daughter's marching band competition in St. Louis. We don't have to call in any special outside support, although sometimes we do invite outside preachers just because it's good and we like them.

This is how it should be, in my opinion. We have inflated the role of pastor in the wrong way in our communities, and part of what I've been working on is moving in different ways that are more anarchist and distributed.

This has been one of the things that I've really leaned into over the past few years —equipping people to preside at the meal and to preach so that there isn't this sense among us that somehow worship can only be hosted when ordained pastors are there.

Try this instead: People join in praise to show the world who they are and whose they are. This is a better definition of the church than the current statement in the Lutheran confessions.

Nanci's sermon sprung from her interaction with the translation notes from the creator of the Women's Lectionary, Wil Gafney, who said in her commentary that the text was familiar to her because of its frequent use in the black church of her youth. She admitted, honestly, that as a white Christian she did not share that same experience.

Then she faithfully brought that ancient text into conversation with a horrible and poignant moment in the history of America, the lynching of Emmett Till. Then she spoke the gospel into that and spoke truth, naming that all lives can't matter until Black Lives Matter. And that health care can't be health care until it's also health care for trans kids.

One of the moms on the marching band trip with me this week mentioned that she'd heard how much our congregation had gone through because of the split and because of our commitment to standing in solidarity with LGBTQIA Christians.

And that's true. And we're very, very different from those years ago. It's like, I've been the pastor of multiple congregations in the same place while maintaining certain kinds of unusual continuity.

I still try to figure out how I'm supposed to be as a pastor who stayed. Nobody stays. Pastors don't stay. When conflict comes the clergy are typically asked by bishops or others to move, and they comply, because honestly fighting through is incredibly hard. It's virtually the hardest thing I've done.

I do not know another pastor who went through a split like ours and stayed. And I've asked around.

I worry that the pastors who leave risk repeating in their career a careful maintenance of always tenuous "peace."

But that's just not what we've done at GSLC.

What has emerged over these last few years: I now inhabit a space as a pastor where I get to walk alongside this congregation as it expresses a way of being in the world that I love.

It's no longer that the congregation must have me here in order for that identity to be part of who it is. Rather I get to align my identity and challenge myself and the congregation to keep exploring what it means to live faithfully in the way of Jesus.

It's a hard won (and always still tenuous) but freeing moment we're in, and the bonus is the beauty of all these people sharing the gifts of the Spirit in community.

OCTOBER 2ND

I think the average Anglo churchgoer lacks awareness of the difference in distance minority Christians have to travel to all meet at "the one table."

Last Sunday when Ozark Atolls hosted a thank you luncheon for our congregation, I mentioned during the sermon how important it was for our congregation to simply attend because the Marshallese have traveled so much farther, so very far, to prepare an amazing meal of their own foods and simply thank us (a thanks we hardly deserve, given all of our complicity in the harm done to the Marshallese Islands from nuclear testing and climate change).

I think we often think of nuclear testing and climate change and other systemic evils as far off things about which we have little control. And in a way that's true.

But in a local congregation the decision whether to help repair the damage done to other communities begins not with big social justice gestures but small steps, small steps like attending a lunch to which you are invited.

A couple of members in our congregation (very active ones, the kind who show up every Sunday and weekdays too) mentioned that they had not planned to attend the lunch because they didn't deserve a thank you or because honestly Marshallese food is foreign to them, and they don't have a taste for it.

The message about the different distances traveling to the one table changed their minds, and they came, even if they didn't know how to eat the food and even if they were afraid they didn't deserve a thank you meal.

I know now from long experience that cultures coming together is hard work on both sides. Our Marshallese neighbors don't necessarily want to come into predominately Anglo spaces all the time either. We all tend toward our own, for a variety of reasons from simple comfort to habit to embarrassment or basic shyness.

What many Christians who have not traveled into other cultures may not know is how central hospitality is to other peoples. This isn't to say that Anglo Christians lack hospitality altogether, but our hospitality is largely optional and often tepid. I've visited many Anglo households where I wasn't even offered a glass of water.

By comparison, when I have lived in Eastern Europe and spent a day grape picking at a family garden, or visited places like a Druze village or Crow Indigenous community or a Swahili congregation, there is an elaborate process for hospitality that verges on the obligatory (this is expected, we aren't doing what we should do if we don't do this) mixed with unadulterated joy (it is so amazing to get to welcome this person/these people to our community).

This is one reason among many why missionaries often receive long training before spending time in another culture. There are approaches to accompanying other cultures that are more or less moral, more or less effective, and at a baseline there are ways to be prepared for cross-cultural immersion that facilitate those crossing the culture to feel more ready.

But when cultures come to us, when they arrived right in the neighborhoods where we live, the signposts for cross-cultural immersion are put up in our front yard. You don't have to book a flight or get a passport. There's no six-month language tutorial. It's just suddenly, you find that your culture is layered in and with another culture, and it is the tiny decisions (I will or will not accept the invitation to this potluck) that become the Christian decisions.

This is made even more complicated by the reality that bringing congregations of different ethnicities together is different from sending a few missionaries. When you send missionaries, or do cross-cultural immersion, it's a select few who make the journey.

But when you bring whole congregations together from different cultures, everyone is along for the ride. Everyone plays a part, even if that part is simply a willingness to try taro for the first time or wait patiently for an event to start when you thought you'd be heading to Starbucks after worship.

I admire those parishioners who have helped me understand what a challenge it is travel the distance we're asking them to travel to meet our Marshallese neighbors. I admire even more our Marshallese neighbors who have had to travel so far, so very far, to meet us where we are. They have traveled so much farther down the road to greet us warmly than we have a right to expect.

I invite anyone reading this to consider our local journey a synecdoche for the whole. *Mutatis mutandi* every community meeting another one across ethnic boundaries and with massive justice disparities between them is going to encounter these struggles and challenges, and it will rarely be the massive righteous gestures that make for healing. It will be the small decisions of showing up, exercising patience, willingness to try things, simple caring, that will make for healing.

And all of this, interestingly enough, IS the gospel in action, because the entire gospel of Jesus Christ articulated in the New Testament hinges around a key concept, Christ's bringing together Jews and Gentiles: "For Jesus is our peace; in his flesh he has made both groups into one and has broken down the dividing wall, that is, the hostility between us" (Ephesians 2:14).

Our entire walk as Christians can be evaluated based on the extent to which we participate in Christ's continuing breaking down of those walls. And some of us have the responsibility of traveling farther than others, if there is going to be true equity and peace.

If you wish to work for racial healing in your communities, start here.

APPENDIX II

WHY I WISH CHURCHES DIDN'T NEED TO START NON-PROFITS

I f you know me very well, this post may come as a surprise. You might think, *He's started multiple nonprofits, partners with many others, and is right now opening a conversation for yet another one. What the what?*

So I won't bury the lede. I have a specific reason I wish churches didn't have to start so many nonprofits. It's because I think most things addressed by such nonprofits would be better addressed by federal and state social services.

In other words, give me a New New Deal rather than a proliferation of non-profits.

We shouldn't have to form nonprofits to provide housing for the homeless: the state should do that. Same for ensuring everyone has food, has access to quality health care, receives all the support and resources they need if they arrive here as an immigrant or refugee; and so on.

Sometimes there is a lot of negative chatter about government bureaucracy, but I consider most of that chatter libertarian and capitalist propaganda. Libertarians falsely assume everyone is best off fending for themselves, and capitalists resist any structures that would place proper regulations and counterpoint to the so-called "free" market.

But really, every org has a structure. The point isn't the size of an org but how well it is run. And orgs at the appropriate scale can do what small orgs in aggregate simply cannot and do more efficiently.

Sociologist Robert Wuthnow once calculated that each church in the US, even the tiny ones, would have to add $700,000 to their budget to cover the services currently provided by the government: food stamps, Medicaid, public housing, etc. I highly doubt most churches would be ready to offer the kinds of services needed to privately replace the public social safety net.

Federal funding for social support works. Food stamps work. Single payer health coverage works. Public housing works.

So my first issue with nonprofits: they are a stop-gap measure we keep implementing because we haven't as-of-yet gathered the political will as a nation to vote in leaders who will establish an actual social safety net that guarantees access to the basics of human life.

And don't even get me stated on a Universal Basic Income, which would change everything.

So those of us who start or donate to or support or run nonprofits do so only out of a problematic necessity: there are no better options and we need to get people into shelter because it's freezing out and the kids are hungry.

Once we've created nonprofits, we rightly celebrate them. They do amazing things. But then we turn that itself into a cultural churn, what some have labeled the "nonprofit industrial complex."

The nonprofit industrial complex (NPIC) refers to **the eclectic collection of privatized nonprofits that provide social service, usually with financial aid from corporations and the government.** This complex has become one of the largest economies in the world, and because it is haphazardly organized yet large, it doesn't alway serve real justice and equality in our communities (see, for example, *The Revolution Will Not Be Funded*).

Why? Well, if you have an entire network of nonprofits all trying to survive and pay their staff and executives, guess what: they all get busy trying to find money. And guess who has ALL the money?

Foundations and rich people and mega corporations.

So now instead of care in community and creativity and so much more designed and led by a democratic or social system, it's all shaped (at least in part) to meet the current ideological whims of foundations and people with money. Sometimes this is good. Other times it's awful. For example, when whole nonprofit systems are developed that help provide shelter in communities, and then the big grant giving agencies decide they aren't interested in housing anymore, but instead are more interested in art.

In the end, I wish we didn't need to create non-profits because there would be no need. Once we are creating non-profits, it means some of us, with the best of intentions, are having to insert ourselves as "patron" or helper into situations where those being helped on certain levels are not empowered to design the systems of support for themselves.

In the meantime, we can apply this critical insight about the problems of non-profits to run the non-profits we do have to start in ways that are as empowering and mutual as possible.

Some notes on how and why to start a nonprofit ...

1. Don't. Do a wide-ranging survey to see if anyone else is doing what it is you want yours to do. If they are, go support that.
2. If after long analysis you realize no one else is doing it, then maybe get a group together and discuss starting one.
3. Now ask yourself: would it be better if a government agency did this? If they aren't, why not?

4. Vote. Advocate. Ask city council members and state legislatures and senators and congresspeople to make change.

5. Okay, you still think you need to start the non-profit. Find a good lawyer who is a friend to help you file all the paperwork. It's not that hard.

6. Find big donors. You're going to need them.

7. Keep meeting and meeting and persisting. Until you hire actual staff, starting a non-profit will become a half to full time job for multiple people. This could be why churches start so many. They have staff resources who can shift some of their time, and networks to recruit volunteers and form teams.

8. Learn how to research and write grants. You'll be doing this a lot.

9. Go back to #1.

10. Go back to #3.

11. If you have funding and you have a board and are now a non-profit, access great resources for board function to learn how to run a non-profit board. I recommend BoardSource.

12. Commit to an excellent relationship between the executive director and the board. This is crucial.

13. Don't drift from your mission.

14. Keep the non-profit about what it is about.

~

That's enough of that. Just one last story. I had a leadership team that met for coffee once a week back around 2014. I made a list for one of our meetings of some things I wanted to do that year. One of them was to start a refugee resettlement agency. When the group looked at the list, they all agreed that was too big and to aim for one of the more realistic items on the list.

By the end of the year, I'd started a refugee resettlement agency.

So maybe 15 is: Make some lists, talk with friends, then don't listen to them... :)

Final note, this post was entirely non-religious, and yet somehow it's central to how I think about church in relationship to the world.

FOR FURTHER READING
INCITE! Women of Color Against Violence, *The Revolution Will Not Be Funded: Beyond the Non-Profit Industrial Complex*, Duke University Press, 2017.

INDEX

Made in the USA
Coppell, TX
08 November 2024

39874958R00187